Working with Your Realms & Your Realm Angels

Maximizing Heaven's Resources for Your Life

Working with Your Realms Series

By

Dr. Ron M. Horner

with Dr. Robert Rodich & Jeremy Friedman

Working with Your Realms & Your Realm Angels

Maximizing Heaven's Resources for Your Life

Working with Your Realms Series

By

Dr. Ron M. Horner

with Dr. Robert Rodich & Jeremy Friedman

LifeSpring Publishing
PO Box 5847
Pinehurst, North Carolina 28374, USA
www.RonHorner.com

Working With Your Realms & Your Realm Angels

Maximizing Heaven's Resources for Your Life

Copyright © 2024 Dr. Ron M. Horner with Dr. Robert Rodich & Jeremy Friedman

Scripture is taken from the New King James Version®. Copyright © 1982 by Thomas Nelson. Used by permission. All rights reserved. (Unless otherwise noted.)

Scripture quotations marked (NIV) are taken from THE HOLY BIBLE, NEW INTERNATIONAL VERSION®. Copyright© 1973, 1978, 1984, 2011 by Biblica, Inc.™. Used by permission of Zondervan.

Scripture quotations are taken from the Holy Bible, New Living Translation (NLT), copyright © 1996, 2004, 2007, 2013, 2015 by Tyndale House Foundation. Used by permission of Tyndale House Publishers, Inc., Carol Stream, Illinois 60188. All rights reserved.

Scripture quotations marked (MESSAGE) are taken from THE MESSAGE, copyright © 1993, 2002, 2018 by Eugene H. Peterson. Used by permission of NavPress, represented by Tyndale House Publishers. All rights reserved.

Scripture marked (TPT) is taken from The Passion Translation Copyright © 2017, 2018 by Passion & Fire Ministries, Inc. Used by permission. All rights reserved. ThePassionTranslation.com

Scripture marked (THE MIRROR) is taken from The Mirror Study Bible by Francois du Toit. Copyright © 2021 All Rights Reserved. Used by permission of The Author.

All rights reserved. This book is protected by the copyright laws of the United States of America. It may not be copied or reprinted for commercial gain or profit. The use of short quotations or occasional page copying for personal, or group study is permitted and encouraged. Permission will be granted upon request.

Requests for bulk sales discounts, editorial permissions, or other information should be addressed to:

LifeSpring Publishing
PO Box 5847
Pinehurst, NC 28374 USA

Additional copies available at RonHorner.com

ISBN 13 TP: 978-1-953684-42-4
ISBN 13 eBook: 978-1-953684-43-1

Cover Design by Darian Horner Design
(www.darianhorner.com)
Image: 123rf.com #117973608, #136535027

First Edition: July 2024

10 9 8 7 6 5 4 3 2 1 0

Printed in the United States of America

Table of Contents

Acknowledgments i

Foreword iii

Characters in this Book v

Preface vii

Section 1 Personal Realms **1**

   Chapter 1 The Necessity for Richness & Purity 3

   Chapter 2 Creating a Cooperation
Between Your Realms 7

   Chapter 3 Joined & Knit Together 23

   Chapter 4 How the Past & Present
Affect the Future 31

   Chapter 5 Quantum:
The Purest Form of Intimacy 37

   Chapter 6 What Are You Hiding? 45

   Chapter 7 What is Joy? 49

Section 2 Quantum Realms **55**

   Chapter 8 Advanced Sonship Technology 57

Chapter 9 A New Design for the Human Body 67

Chapter 10 Engaging with Quantum Realms 77

Chapter 11 The Quantum Emotional Realm 89

Chapter 12 The Quantum Heart Realm 91

Chapter 13 The Quantum Essence Realm 103

Chapter 14 Working with Frequencies
from the Quantum Essence Realm 113

Chapter 15 Dimensional Transformation 127

Chapter 16 Quantum Realm Angels 133

Chapter 17 Cleansing Our Realms
& Heavenly Alignment 139

Section 3 Practicing a Lifestyle 145

Chapter 18 Separating from the Tree
of the Knowledge of Good & Evil 147

Chapter 19 The Three Books 153

Chapter 20 It's a Season of Portals 161

Chapter 21 Ordering, Conquering, & Governing .. 169

Chapter 22 Living Trans-dimensionally 179

Chapter 23 Being Trans-dimensional 187

Chapter 24 Mastering the Mind 201

Chapter 25 Wielding the Sword of Resolve 211

Chapter 26 Maximizing "As If It Never Were" 215

Chapter 27 Script for Aligning Your Realms 229

Appendix 237

Silver & Gold Capture Bags 239
Works Cited 257
Description 259
About the Authors 261
About the Contributors 263
Other Books 265

Acknowledgments

The hosts of Heaven are to be acknowledged first, for without their input, they would not be fulfilling their redemption, and we would be missing much revelation that we need in this time.

Dr. Robert Rodich and Jeremy Friedman are also to be commended for their input into this book as they each contributed several chapters. Flavia Diaz and Author Rachael Testa are also to be acknowledged for their contributions to the book. This was truly a collaborative effort by many individuals both on this side of Heaven and on the other side.

Thanks also to the LifeSpring team in every realm. We appreciate all you bring to the table to extend the Kingdom.

———— ∞ ————

Foreword

Let me say I'm very excited about Dr. Horner's new work on our realms (body, soul, and spirit). Dr. Horner is totally committed to putting on paper only what Heaven really wants us to know, knowing that traditional Christianity will offer little support.

As this journey intensifies, it will become critical that every possible part of our nature be cleansed, restored, and repurposed for the work of God's Kingdom. It is increasingly looking like we all are going to play a larger role in how things play out in the future.

The contents of this book are likely to be next-level stuff, so I'd pay careful attention. Getting our realms lined up and fully functional will likely unleash a wave of power and victory, the likes of which all creation has been groaning for some time.

God's power, purpose, and design are being released in heavenly waves all around us; however, they must be released and imparted into the fabric of Earth's design. Picture it as something seeking a perfect harmonic delivery system to find a place of rest and then release. You and I are that delivery system if we have worked to synchronize our realms (especially our souls).

Put your seatbelt on and get ready for the next step.

– Dr. Robert Rodich

———— ∞ ————

Characters in this Book

In this book, we introduce you to several entities who assisted us in its writing:

Adina – Ron Horner's wife, a psalmist and minstrel.

Alicia – a woman in white who serves as our Personnel Advisor.

Bartholomew – A man in white who assisted us.

David – David Porter III is Lead Apostle of Sandhills Ecclesia and an accountant on our team.

Einstein (Albert) – now a man in white who often tutors us.

Ezekiel – the Chief Angel over LifeSpring.

Enoch – a man in white mentioned in Genesis and Jude.

Gloria – a woman in white who assists us.

Jerry – a man in white with whom Flavia Diaz engaged.

Jesus – He needs no introduction.

John – the New Testament apostle.

Joy – an entity to bring the power of joy into our lives.

Lydia – a woman in white who assists LifeSpring.

Malcolm – a man in white who often tutors us. He is also the Headmaster of CourtsNet.

Mitchell – a man in white who tutors us.

Peter – the New Testament apostle.

Purity – an angel who assists with bringing purity into the lives of the saints.

Stephanie – my current Executive Assistant.

Wisdom (Spirit of Wisdom) – one of the seven spirits of God.

──── ∞ ────

Preface

In the spring of 2023, Heaven began unveiling some new revelations that would forever change the lives of the leadership of our ministry as well as our clients and families. To start this journey, I became acquainted with Dr. Robert Rodich, a naturopath and retired pastor. He shared a little bit of a revelation he had, and my seer stepped into that revelation, and Heaven built upon it.

That understanding opened a whole new world and new information concerning a class of angels referred to (by me, at least) as Realm Angels. That will be explained more as we go forward in this book. This information seemed to simply add to the revelation in my book *Living Spirit Forward,* which has helped thousands have language for what Holy Spirit had been speaking to them about for a long time.

Personally, I do not believe that we have all the revelation that Heaven wants to download to us, and I believe we can create a place within our hearts for more revelation to come. For that to occur, however, will require some adjustments to our thinking processes and a willingness to embrace new information and new insights that will take us farther than we have ever been. We also must be willing to be wrong about some of our beliefs and preconceptions. I have had to face that many times over the last few years.

The good news is that Heaven has given us a simple prophetic act to assist us in helping our souls receive this revelation into our lives. Many times, our soul, out of its own insecurity and protective mechanisms, will reject revelation because, to its mind, it does not make sense. The fact is revelation rarely makes sense to our natural mind. Our spirit is the first repository of revelation from Heaven, not our soul; however, our soul has been so accustomed to providing the filter to information that it thinks it is the soul's responsibility to receive revelation first. Yet, when it relinquishes that duty to our spirit, our soul becomes much more settled in the entire process.

Do you remember when Jesus was speaking concerning wineskins?

> *And no one puts new wine into old wineskins; or else the new wine will burst the wineskins and be spilled, and the wineskins will be ruined. (Luke 5:37)*

Another solution also exists. Apply oil to the old wineskin, and it will become pliable again.

Here is the simple prophetic act to enlarge your soul:

- Speak to your soul, telling it that everything will be OK.
- Begin using your hands to stretch something. Imagine you are in a large balloon and need to stretch it from the inside. Begin pressing in every direction on the sides of the balloon.
- Request the oil of ease be applied to your soul.

You will sense an ease coming to your soul in receiving the revelation Heaven wants to pour out. Throughout the reading of this book, you may need to pause to enlarge your soul periodically.

Most of us have been taught that our soul was at war with our spirit. It does not have to be that way. Paul did say the carnal mind was at enmity against our spirit. To understand what Paul was saying, we need to read the passage in context:

> *¹ There is therefore now no condemnation to those who are in Christ Jesus, who do not walk according to the flesh,* **but according to the Spirit.**
>
> *² For the law of the Spirit of life in Christ Jesus has made me free from the law of sin and death.*

³ For what the law could not do in that it was weak through the flesh, God did by sending His own Son in the likeness of sinful flesh, on account of sin: He condemned sin in the flesh,

*⁴ that the righteous requirement of the law might be fulfilled in us <u>who do not walk according to the flesh</u> **but according to the Spirit.***

*⁵ For those who live according to the flesh set their minds on the things of the flesh, but **those who live according to the Spirit, the things of the Spirit.***

⁶ For to be carnally minded is death, but <u>to be spiritually minded is life and peace.</u>¹

⁷ Because the carnal mind is enmity against God; for it is not subject to the law of God, nor indeed can be.

⁸ So then, <u>those who are in the flesh cannot please God.</u>

*⁹ But **you are not in the flesh but in the Spirit, if indeed the Spirit of God dwells in you.** Now if anyone does not have the Spirit of Christ, he is not His.*

¹⁰ And if Christ is in you, the body is dead because of sin, but <u>the Spirit is life because of righteousness.</u>

---

[1] The spiritual mind is in the Quantum Heart.

> *¹¹ But if the Spirit of Him who raised Jesus from the dead dwells in you, He who raised Christ from the dead will also give life to your mortal bodies <u>through His Spirit who dwells in you</u>. (Romans 8:1-11) (Emphasis added)*

Paul was simply explaining that you can live out of one of two realms: the realm dictated by the desires of the flesh (our soul and body), or we can be under the guidance of Holy Spirit. I choose the latter and believe that you do, too, or you would not be reading this book.

As you progress in this book, you will be open to new and/or fuller understandings. If you come to a spot where your soul is giving some kickback, ask, "What is the source of the kickback? The Tree of Life? Or the Tree of the Knowledge of Good and Evil?" Heaven wants us to disconnect from the latter tree and connect *ONLY* to the Tree of Life. We will talk about how to do that later in this book. Living from the Tree of Life is where the presence of God is!

Many are surprised to learn that each of their realms has a voice, can speak to you, and can help you work with them more effectively. Learning to engage with them will bless your life immensely.

As you read this book, you will be encouraged to engage with yourself in ways you may never have considered. I promise—it will not be a boring journey.

This edition does not fully explain aligning our realms, but it is a starting point. Begin here and watch your life change. Further volumes will cover the new discoveries from Heaven to Earth.

As you read this book, some chapters are from our various authors or contributors. Otherwise, I, Dr. Ron Horner, am the author.

———— ∞ ————

Section 1
Personal Realms

Section I

Mental Residue

Chapter 1
The Necessity
for Richness & Purity

The sounds we were hearing flowed from the giant harp in front of us as we engaged with Heaven. The melody was very calming as we listened to it. We realized that a large gathering of people was around us, and they were also playing music. The melody was pure.

Malcolm, a man in white who often tutors us, reminded us that we could lean into the richness of the frequency when we stepped into Heaven.

We enjoyed the richness of the purity of the sounds we were hearing. Malcolm reminded us that the key was purity. As he said that, we could see the entity that is Purity. Many things we thought were verbs or nouns in the Bible are actual entities that we can engage, and we can receive what it is that they are.

We were instructed by Purity to tell our audience to engage Heaven in the richness and in the purity of what Heaven is. Many who are just learning about stepping into Heaven have a fear of the demonic, so as they are stepping in, they forget that no demons exist in Heaven. Nothing but purity and the richness of Heaven is present, and they can take that within themselves.

We need to remember the covenant. The covenant explains why and how we can receive the richness, purity, and melody of Heaven. We don't have to trust in ourselves; we can trust in the process as we step in as sons.

As we come into deeper revelation, Heaven continually brings us back to the basics to prepare our hearts—the sons' hearts.

We will always return to the richness of Heaven's simplicity. As we move from glory to glory, from revelation to revelation, there will be constant reminders of its **simplicity. That is how the sons will be able to handle the revelation.**

There will be constant reminders of the simplicity. That is how the sons will be able to handle the revelation.

Richness and purity are necessary for us as sons as we step into deeper revelation.

Malcolm reminded us that Purity is present because that is what she is bringing to the body. We have asked for innocence to be restored, and she is bringing purity back to the people. Purity can bring purity back into people's lives when it is given away or stolen. It is part of redemption—as if it never were.

Jesus even defined purity for us in Mark 7:14-16:

14 When He had called all the multitude to Himself, He said to them, 'Hear Me, everyone, and understand:

15 There is nothing that enters a man from outside which can defile him; but the things which come out of him, those are the things that defile a man.

16 If anyone has ears to hear, let him hear!'

Earlier in the same chapter, Jesus discussed the wrong concept of purity held by religious scholars. They thought purity was defined by ceremonial washings and other rituals.

20 And He said, 'What comes out of a man, that defiles a man.

21 For from within, out of the heart of men, proceed evil thoughts, adulteries, fornications, murders, 22 thefts, covetousness, wickedness, deceit, lewdness, an evil eye, blasphemy, pride, foolishness. ²³ All these evil things come from within and defile a man.' (Mark 7:20-23)[2]

Because we have all committed those things in sin, we've been doing the clean-up work, and the Father has been introducing us to Purity.

Remember the phrase in Genesis 6:9 where it says,

And Noah was made perfect in his generations.

He didn't have as many generations to clean up, but they proved it could be done.

Returning to the basics is often necessary before we progress to the next thing. The wonderful thing about the revelation we are about to share is that it will further empower us to become more of the sons the Father desires.

———— ∞ ————

---

[2] When the heart is controlled by the carnal mind, it can only draw from an improper source.

Chapter 2
Creating a Cooperation Between Your Realms

As you begin reading this chapter, you want to be sure your spirit is forward, and your soul is settled in a cooperative position. It may also be a good time to enlarge your soul so you can receive the revelation contained herein. The complete script that is updated from the one in this chapter can be found in the last chapter of this book.

One thing that surprises many people who do this exercise is that each of their realms—spirit, soul, and body—has a voice, and that voice longs to be heard. Our realms want input into our lives and are grateful when we recognize them and give them the opportunity to help us.

Stephanie, my Executive Assistant, recently asked her body what it needed, and it told her that it needed better nutrition. Finally, it said to her, "Eat a salad, lady!" Surprised by the response but also cognizant of the truth of what it was saying, Stephanie obeyed, and I observed her eating a salad soon thereafter.

To maximize the benefits of this book, we need to begin by calling our spirit forward. Begin by following this simple pattern:

- Speak to your soul and instruct it to sit back and rest and not block what is coming from our spirit to our heart.
- Speak to your spirit and call it to come forward and be dominant at this time.

You may sense a subtle shift—almost like you are putting a car into drive from park or neutral.

Now, take a moment and enlarge your soul. Do the prophetic act of stretching it to enlarge it. Request the oil of ease to be given to your soul.

You may want to pray in the spirit for a moment as well. Praying in the spirit is one way that we build a structure to contain revelation (See 1 Corinthians 14). What size structure do you want to build?

Stephanie and I had been engaging Heaven for new levels of freedom. As part of that journey, I met Dr. Robert Rodich. He had some things to say that I want to share with you:

Scripture says we are made in God's image, but what image?[3]

> *So God created man in His own image; in the image of God He created him; male and female He created them. (Genesis 1:27)*

God is three in one, and so are we. We have a physical body, a soul, and a spirit. Before man's fall, all three parts operated with incredible harmony and synchronicity.

Most agree that our mind, will, and emotions reside in the soul. However, I have discovered that **each part of our nature has its own mind, will, and emotions.**

Each part of our nature has its own mind, will, and emotions.

Because we start out being so soul-dominated, that domination makes it appear our other two parts get their voice and personality entirely from the soul. Yet when we read all the scripture texts that address this subject, none say it is only the soul that has these attributes.

When this was brought to my attention, I decided to test it. I spoke out loud and

---

[3] Portions from *Moving Toward Sonship* by Dr. Robert Rodich. (LifeSpring Publishing, 2023)

*acknowledged each part of my being for its respective role in making up my whole person, charging each to fulfill its **role in unity and harmony.***

Activating Cooperation

Let's do this right now:

1. Speak out loud.
2. Acknowledge each part of your being for their respective roles in making up your whole person.
- **Spirit**, I acknowledge you and thank you for your role in my being.
- **Soul**, I acknowledge you and thank you for your role in my being.
- **Body**, I acknowledge you and thank you for your role in my being.

Then,

3. Charge each to fulfill their role in <u>unity</u> and <u>harmony</u>.
- **Spirit**, I charge you to fulfill your role in unity and harmony with my soul and body.
- **Soul**, I charge you to fulfill your role in unity and harmony with my spirit and body.
- **Body**, I charge you to fulfill your role in unity and harmony with my spirit and soul.

*I had immediate results, sensing a deep inner stirring and almost a sigh of relief. It was like I could hear my three parts saying, 'He finally gets it!' I went on to realize that each was very excited to be enabled to a **higher standard of functionality and purpose**.*

Your realms will be enabled
to a higher standard
of functionality and purpose.

For the naysayers—no, I didn't feel at that moment, nor do I feel now like I am three different people. Frankly, until I made this declaration, I didn't realize how dysfunctional I really was compared to how things are now. Now my personal spirit is free to see into the heavenly realm, bring those realities to the part of my soul that interprets them for my understanding, and then make that truth available so that my body can manifest it either for my personal benefit or to speak it into reality on planet Earth. This is what sons (daughters) are supposed to do.

...and greater works than these will he do. (John 14:12)

There are those who teach that once we accept Christ as Lord and Savior, we have everything we need—which is true according to 2 Peter 1:3, which says,

His divine power has given us everything we need for life and godliness through our knowledge of Him who called us by his own glory and goodness.

This verse tells us that we must engage with this. The potential is fully there, yet has it been realized?

A real disconnect occurs when those interpreting scripture cannot distinguish between **potential** *and* **practice. Just because something is available to us doesn't mean we have activated it or know how to use it.**

Knowing we are three-part beings and each part of us has a role is vital as we compare our present situation against the possibilities set forth in God's Word. **We may find things that need to be put out of each part of us so that those things the Father has put into us can rise to their proper place.** *The goal of this process is so the person of our Savior assimilates himself into us in a way that we are less self, more Him and then more of who we really are. The natural-minded person will never get this; however, it becomes ever clearer as we move through this process.*

In 1 Corinthians 2:11-13, we read:

[11] For what man knows the things of a man, except the spirit of man which is in

him? Even so the things of God knows no man, but the Spirit of God.

¹² Now we have received, not the spirit of the world, but the spirit which is of God; that we might know the things that are freely given to us of God.

¹³ Which things also we speak, not in the words which man's wisdom teaches, but which the Holy Spirit teaches; comparing spiritual things with spiritual.

Add to this that each member of the Trinity seems to take responsibility for each part of us and **delights in showing special love and direction**.

Father oversees our spirit,
Jesus, our soul,
and the Holy Spirit our body.

---

*And the very God of peace sanctify you wholly, and I pray God your **whole spirit and soul and body** be preserved blameless unto the coming of our Lord Jesus Christ. (1 Thessalonians 5:23) (Emphasis added)*

*What? know ye not that <u>your **body** is the temple of the **Holy Ghost**</u>, which is in you, which ye have of God, and ye are not your own? (1 Corinthians 6:19)*

Holy Spirit—oversees our body

Let this mind be in you, which was also in Christ Jesus. (Philippians 2:5)

Jesus—oversees our mind/soul

*Now we have received, not the spirit of the world, but the **spirit which is of God**; that we might know the things that are freely given to us of God. (I Corinthians 2:12)*

Father—oversees our spirit

*As one who has operated well in the gifts of the Holy Spirit and seer giftings, I must say that I have long been able to distinguish each member of the Godhead, speaking individually as an inner voice within me. However, **when I verbally asked the Father, Jesus, and the Holy Spirit to exercise dominion over the corresponding part of my nature, I started to hear all three of them simultaneously.***

Holy Union

*I share this as something for you to look forward to. I call this **Holy Union**. This union is available* *to encourage us to the greatest possible intimacy with our very creator and a new level of power and purpose. This explains why it seems that every evil force in the universe works overtime to keep us from getting to this place.*

Creating Holy Union

*Verbally ask Father,
Jesus, and Holy Spirit
to exercise dominion over the
corresponding part of our nature:*

Father, I invite you to exercise dominion over my spirit.

Jesus, I invite you to exercise dominion over my soul.

Holy Spirit, I invite you to exercise dominion over my body.

∞

1 Corinthians 12:17 says:

If the **whole body** were an eye, where would be the hearing? If the whole were hearing, where would be the smelling?

Whole = complete, entire; body = the sound whole

James 3:2 tells us:

For we all stumble in many things. If anyone does not stumble in word, he is a perfect man, able also to bridle the whole body.

Journaling

This segment is from journaling I conducted during the early days of learning about this:

You noticed the wording of 'whole body' in the Scriptures. When you see that, it speaks of all that is contained within the physical form. Because you have a body, you also have a soul and a spirit. When the spirit leaves, the body dies. The soul has no more purpose on this plane after the body dies, for it was the interface for the 3-D realm and Heaven. Your soul lets your body know what it is experiencing from Heaven and translates it in a fashion that is acceptable. Your soul also protected you from overloads coming from the 3-D realm. It had a specific purpose while the body lived.

Although songs speak of the soul and 'saving your soul,' you aren't really saving it; you are helping your spirit come alive to who you really are. Your spirit must be awakened to its destiny and purpose, which starts with salvation.

Without that process, people's spirits are typically not awakened. New Agers awaken it to a degree, but they do so from the Tree of the Knowledge of Good and Evil. It must be awakened from the Tree of Life. Everything else is futile.

Most songs and sermons about saving one's soul are based on incorrect or incomplete information. **As an awakened son, your soul is being transformed as you live from your spirit and find its proper place in the equation.**

Yes, you do have angels assigned to the three basic realms. They are typically unemployed until you <u>awaken and commission your realms to work in unity and harmony to fulfill the plan of the Father.</u> **Once that is done and they are acknowledged, then those angels go to work fulfilling your destiny on a whole new level. They awaken you to sonship realities.**

Realm Angels awaken you
to sonship realities.

They awaken you to who you **can be** and **who you really are**. That can happen on some level without commissioning your realms, but it works better when they do. The Scripture in 1 Thessalonians 5:-22-23 speaks to this:

[22] Abstain from every form of evil.

> *²³ Now may the God of peace Himself sanctify you completely; and may your whole **spirit**, **soul**, and **body** be preserved blameless at the coming of our Lord Jesus Christ.*

Or,

> *²² Distance yourselves immediately from every practice remotely related to the fruit of the 'I-am-not-tree,' which is the typical exhausting law of works system.*
>
> *²³ There, away from any effort of your own, discover how the God of perfect peace, who fused you skillfully into oneness—just like a master craftsman would dovetail a carpentry joint—has personally perfected and sanctified the entire harmony of your being without your help. He has restored the detailed default settings. **You were re-booted to fully participate in the life of your design, in your spirit, soul, and body in blameless innocence in the immediate presence of our Lord Jesus Christ**. (Emphasis mine) (THE MIRROR)*

Understanding how the Godhead works in concert with man's whole being is helpful for understanding who is speaking to you.

The nuances of each voice are important to learn and will come over time for most who are *pursuing these realities. It is the desire of the Father to bring forth these understandings so the Body of Christ can become what He has envisioned from before time. You are simply experiencing sonship realities as you do these things. Don't despair from the journey. Keep activating and implementing the revelation you receive. Let it bring forth life in you—life abundantly.*

Speaking to Our Realms

Some have trouble with the idea of speaking to the spirit, soul, or body, saying, "I'll just speak to the Holy Spirit." Have they forgotten that Jesus spoke with Moses and Elijah, Abraham spoke with the men in white who came to meet with him, Mary spoke to Gabriel, and others throughout scripture spoke to whomever God sent to them? It is arrogant to say we will "only speak to Holy Spirit."

If you needed work done on your house and you called a company to give an estimate of the repairs needed, but instead of the company owner coming to meet with you, he/she sent a trusted employee to take care of the situation—would it not be arrogant of you to say, "I won't speak with you because you're not the boss?"

Yes, it would. Refusing to speak to anyone but the boss would also disrespect the employee and the boss. Are you the expert? Not likely.

Remember that religious spirits always want to dictate the rules of engagement. Submitted spirits will receive whomever Heaven sends.

Each of our realms has a voice and has a specific part to play in enriching our lives.

Allow Heaven to make the decisions on who to engage with.

Otherwise, you have stepped into a place of judgment against the Father. Remember, the rich man in Luke 12:19 spoke to his soul. David also spoke to his soul in Psalm 11:1, Psalm 35:3, Psalm 42:5, 11, 43:5, as well as other places. He spoke specifically to his soul in Psalm 103:22 and 104:1, 35, and 146:1.

David understood that his soul needed instruction, direction, and comfort. He speaks of the soul over one hundred times in the Psalms.

Think about it. How often have you spoken to your body to get up and get out of bed? We speak to our realms regularly. Why not do so with intentionality?

In Proverbs 24:12, we are told that our soul knows what is going on within it. It would behoove us to listen to our realms. We may be surprised by what we learn.

———— ∞ ————

Chapter 3
Joined & Knit Together

Stephanie and I had been asking for revelation on the Realm Angels, so we accessed the Library of Revelation to learn more. Stephanie's Realm Angels appeared in front of her. They were to be our tutors. The soul angel and the body angel were the most predominant at this point. Her spirit angel was some distance away from her. It was pointed out that the body and soul angels had things to teach us first.

They pointed out to us that in Matthew 6:33 we read, *"...seek first the Kingdom of God,"* and that, when we seek the Kingdom, we could seek them out because they are part of the Kingdom.

The soul angel reminded us of the scripture, *"...a house divided against itself cannot stand."*[4] When our house is divided, we cannot stand. These angels are

---

[4] Mark 3:25

designed to work together so that we can stand and be established in the things of the Kingdom.

When reading that verse, understand the converse of it—a house united CAN stand. "A three-fold cord is not easily broken," (Ecclesiastes 4:12)—with the three parts of you knit or wound tightly together you are better able to stand and withstand various challenges and assaults.

> ¹⁵ *but, speaking the truth in love, may grow up in all things into Him who is the head—Christ—*
>
> ¹⁶ *from whom the **whole body**, **joined** and **knit together** by what every joint supplies, according to the effective working by which every part does its share, causes growth of the body for the edifying of itself in love. (Ephesians 4:15-16)*

When verses use the phrase "whole body" it refers to all that is contained within the realm of the body which includes the spirit and soul. This passage shows that they can and should be **joined** and **knit together**.

Ephesians 2:20-22, speaking of us, says,

> ²⁰ *having been built on the foundation of the apostles and prophets, with Christ Jesus Himself as the [chief] Cornerstone,*
>
> ²¹ *in whom the whole structure is **joined together**, and it continues [to increase] growing into a holy temple in the Lord [a sanctuary*

dedicated, set apart, and sacred to the presence of the Lord].

Colossians 2:19 reminds us:

*...from whom all the body, nourished and **knit together** by joints and ligaments, **grows with the increase that is from God**. (Emphasis added)*

With our realms working
in harmony with one another,
we will grow through an increase
that comes from God.

Our soul is not kicking against us, it is being a bridge and not a gatekeeper. Our body is flowing with the flow of Heaven and it is able to receive, not only from our soul, but also from our spirit directly.

In Him [and in fellowship with one another] you also are being built together into a dwelling place of God in the Spirit. (Ephesians 2:22)

We want to be a recognizable dwelling place of God in the realm of the spirit, not just in our spirit realm. Father has supplied angels who specialize in working in our personal realms—that is their sole duty. The Realm Angels look different than other angels; their wings are different, and they glow. Often, they will glow in various colors—one minute pink, another minute purple, and so on. It is part of their variety and beauty.

> *Realm Angels are responsible for removing residue and debris that has impacted your spirit, soul, or body because of wrong relationships.*

Working in Tandem

In the Library of Revelation, to which we had access, we were sitting at a table with a book in front of us. Printed on the front of it were the words, "What is Tandem?"

> *Tandem is working together of two or more things.*

Stephanie opened the book and read a rhyme, "Tandem is two and one and one and two. Not two in two or one in one and three parts or four and sometimes more."

She turned the page and read, "Seek heavenly tandem constructs." She was then drawn to scripture in Micah 2:13, which, on the surface, she did not understand.

> *Your leader will break out and lead you out of exile, out through the gates of the enemy cities back to your own land. Your king will lead you,*

and the Lord himself will guide you. (Micah 2:13) (NLT)

---
*Your leader is your spirit
working with these angels.*

In the Message translation, it made more sense.

Then I, God, will burst out all confinements and lead them out into the open. They'll follow their king and I'll be out in front leading them. (MESSAGE)

If a house is divided because it is not in unity and harmony and there are fractures with different parts, when it comes back together, it is a whole in unity and harmony. Then you're also in that with Jesus, the Father, and the Holy Spirit. You're coming out of the enemy's camp. He's losing his grip.

The angels wanted her to turn her page.

The angel on her right (her soul angel) was now highlighted and pointed to several scriptures about defiling one's soul. She also heard Ruth's entreaty to Naomi:

[16] But Ruth said: 'Entreat me not to leave you, Or to turn back from following after you; For wherever you go, I will go; And wherever you lodge, I will lodge; Your people shall be my people, And your God, my God.

¹⁷ Where you die, I will die, And there will I be buried. The LORD do so to me, and more also, If anything but death parts you and me.' (Ruth 1:16-17)

They implied to us that where we go, they go. We are NEVER without their presence, whether we recognize them or not—even to the depths of Sheol.

⁷ Where can I go from Your Spirit? Or where can I flee from Your presence?

⁸ If I ascend into Heaven, You are there; If I make my bed in hell, behold, You are there. (Psalms 139:7-8)

Because we have sought this information out as we begin to align the spirit, soul, and body, even the places where the body or the soul has been fractured, it can be rectified.

Realm Angels do not need weapons. Those are for angels of other classes who work specifically with bonds, territories, and dimensions. Because our realms can be fragmented and put into different dimensions, they can work in those areas.

I commission you, body, soul, and spirit angels to work in tandem with one another, in tandem with the Father, the Son, and the Holy Spirit.

You may sense them simply stepping inside of one another. You may sense the energy coming from that.

James 5:16 says:

The effective, fervent prayer of a righteous man avails much.

When all our parts agree with what we are doing, answers can come on a large scale.

This is more than just a group hug. This is them becoming inside one another.

When our soul, body, and spirit become tandem, become one interchangeably, that is tandem totality.[5]

---

[20] *'I do not pray for these alone, but also for those who will believe in Me through their word;*

[21] *that they all **may be one**, as You, Father, are in Me, and I in You; that they also **may be one in Us**, that the world may believe that You sent Me.*

[22] *And the glory which You gave Me I have given them, that they **may be one** just as **We are one**:*

[23] *I in them, and You in Me; that they **may be made perfect in one**, and that the world may*

---

[5] As we will learn later, this is also a form of quantum entanglement.

know that You have sent Me, and have loved them as You have loved Me.' (John 17:20-23)

Jesus prayed this for us. We have often thought He was just praying for the overall unity of the Body of Christ, but now we know He was praying for the unity within each member of the Body of Christ. At the time He prayed this, the Holy Spirit had not come on the scene in the earthly realm. That was to come a few weeks later, on the day of Pentecost. He would be included in the scenario at that time.

The explosive power of this in our lives will be like a ball of energy. The reverberation will be massive. Envision it like a tennis ball being hit with a tennis racket and going out really fast and really far. This is a place of reckoning against the enemy. It is not just a reckoning; it also wrecks the enemy's plans. This is where we can do all things *in* Christ. The oneness—the totality of our spirit, soul, and body with the blood of Jesus and the name of Jesus—will be the reckoning against the enemy, to be the effectual fervent prayers of a righteous man that avail much.

———— ∞ ————

Chapter 4

How the Past & Present Affect the Future

In this engagement with Heaven, Lydia and Gloria both appeared to speak with us. Lydia asked a question, "The past and the present affect the future, or does it?"

We were not sure how to reply so we asked her to expound upon her question. Gloria was holding some files in her arms. She asked, "Do you think these affect the future?"

Stephanie replied saying, "Gloria, my initial thought was that these are things of the past that have been handled in court because of our repentances. Because of those things, is it affecting the future in a good way?"

"Yes," Gloria replied.

Stephanie asked, "But what about those that continue to hold on to the *past* or hold on to the *present?*"

Gloria replied, "There is much to be said about letting go of the past and not staying in the present."

We found ourselves walking into court where Gloria began presenting the files of the past and of the present on behalf of the people that she had been holding.

Stephanie could see the accuser of the brethren come in. It was as if chains were attached to the files, and he was a puppeteer. They looked like strings, but in fact, they were chains attached to all of Gloria's paperwork.

He said he had a legal right because the people, with their mindsets, were holding onto these things instead of letting them go. Then he said, "It's either your righteous verdict or it's not" (meaning, the people represented by the files did not really believe the verdict of the Courts of Heaven). He said those things with a sneer.

We approached the bench and said:

Your Honor, we stand here as ministers of reconciliation on behalf of ourselves, on behalf of those employed by LifeSpring International Ministries, our contractors, our volunteers, our intercessors, and people who trade with us, those who come near and draw near, on their behalf and on ours.

We repent for where we have held on to the past and have stayed in the present instead of moving forward with Heaven and its verdicts that have been rendered on our behalf. We ask for the blood of Jesus here.

We forgive, bless, and release those and their generations as well as our generations, where we have stayed in the past, not wanting to move forward while standing in the present. We are to be looking forward, moving forward.

I ask for the amendment of 'As If It Never Were' and for these chains to be severed.

I request that the impact, ramifications, and consequences of these sins be overturned, nullified, and voided in the Court of Cancellations. I ask for further counsel or your righteous verdict.

Gloria came forward and gave us a key. She said,

> The future waits for the sons of men.

Stephanie continued,

I would like to close the door, Your Honor, on the past and even the present and open the door to the future, the forward momentum, the Kingdom dynamics, and on our behalf as a ministry, that we drop the Tree of the Knowledge of Good and Evil.

We would like a full cancellation of the cycles I see because of the tree.

The Just Judge asked, "Do you know who I am?"

Stephanie replied, "You are I AM."

As she responded, he began commanding the breaking free of all of the cycles of living in the past and the present. She watched the removal of the chains.

Thank you, Holy Spirit. I see you moving here like the wind. Teach us your ways, oh God. Renew a right spirit within all of us. We repent for our egos, for all of those things of the past, and we say yes to moving forward with Your Kingdom.

Petitioning the Court

I would like the holy fire to burn on all of these chains and remove them from our records in time and out of time and every age, realm, and dimension.

Gloria walked up and handed me these files, which no longer had the chains attached, and said,

---
Let the future carry you.

Stephanie immediately heard the scripture,

You shall mount up on wings like eagles; you shall run and not grow weary; you shall walk and not faint.[6]

---

[6] Isaiah 40:31

Continuing her petition, she said,

As a son of God, I ask that this be a bond upon the people and their realms, that the angels bring it to their realms, and that it be recorded for them, for LifeSpring International Ministries, and for all of the entities that belong to it.

Suddenly, Stephanie saw a car crash.

Lydia asked, "Would this not show a picture of where forward momentum has been stopped instantaneously?"

Stephanie replied, "Yes. Immediately I thought, 'This car crash is bad.'"

Lydia remarked, "Think about what just happened here as an immediate disruption of the past and the present."

Stephanie replied, "I want to get us all in that new vehicle and move forward. Thank you for that, Lydia.

We ask for all heavenly disruptors, and I ask the angels to render this. I ask for the unplugging of all those who draw near, work for, contract with, co-labor with, or serve as intercessors and volunteers with LifeSpring. Help them move from the Tree of the Knowledge of Good and Evil, and may they reside in the Tree of Life.

Thank you, Father. Thank you, Jesus, for this opportunity.

Just then, Lydia began dusting debris off Stephanie's shoulder as if she were removing the rest of the past from her.

———— ∞ ————

Chapter 5

Quantum:

The Purest Form of Intimacy

Stephanie asked, "When you hear that the Father has called someone to holiness, what does that mean to you specifically?"

I replied, "I always think of when Samuel's mother was praying for a son and promised to give him to the Lord and was told to never let a razor touch his head. Her future son had been called to holiness."

Stephanie asked, "Is that different now that we are in the New Covenant, with the Holy Spirit and the blood of Jesus?"

I answered, "He, the Father, is the one who makes us holy, but we make the determination to pursue holiness."

Stephanie promptly said, "Well, I make the determination to pursue holiness as the Father has made me holy."

We then requested access to the realms of Heaven and asked, "What do you have, Father?"

Stephanie could see large cinder blocks as if a partial wall were going up. It was longer at the bottom because it was being built.

She asked, "Can someone explain to me what this is?"

Malcolm peeked his head around the corner and asked, "How many walls do you think people have put up in the spirit against the Father?

"Reconciliation is about building bridges and not erecting walls. There is no sure foundation in erecting these kinds of walls against Heaven."

The sure foundation is found in the completeness of one's identity to who they are in Christ.

He said, "Let's talk about spiritual domains."

Malcolm was leaning up against the wall and I asked him, "How can we take this wall down?

"As the people have been moving through generational cleansing, these walls come down."

He took off the first top cinder block and laid it on the ground.

He continued, "Continue through the constructs of time. Generations have been building walls against the Father, not piece by piece—that is the first step."

Stephanie commented, "I see three cinder blocks. It is as if he is going to pull them all off at the same time. How is that done?"

Malcolm replied, "Through the purging of old mindsets and religious thinking, they are dismantled."

Stephanie now could see two cinder blocks. He was about to remove them.

She asked, "How can we remove that one?"

Malcolm explained, "These are here because of the lack of praise and worship, adoration, gratitude, and bestowing upon the Father and the Son the recognition for what has been done."

He pulled that block down and was now standing on top of them.

The first layer of this was the **lack of desire**.

Suddenly, a portal opened. He asked, "Are you ready to go further?"

"Yes. Malcolm, thank you for the initial first steps," we replied. We walked through this portal with him, and we could see that it was a long tunnel, but we saw it moving around us as if it were alive. We opened our eyes and could see no obstructions in front of us. We were in the realm of intimacy.

---

*To understand physics,
you must first understand intimacy.*

He said, "If Father created time and space, would He not have done so in intimacy with time and space?

"When something is lovingly created, there is an intimacy to it. That is why people can walk in the intimacy of the Father because they are in time and space. He created it. The practicality of all of this is to understand it is all relevant. The cry of intimacy far outweighs the building blocks set against time and space.

---

*Quantum is
the purest form of intimacy.*

---

*Without quantum undoing,
the done could never be done.*

"There would be no intimacy with his people. He loves them so much. He can do these things under his constructs without physics.

There could be no intimacy without physics.

"It's all relative." He said, "Chew on that one."

Stephanie replied, "Well, I am going to have to because I have no idea about what you are talking about!"

Malcolm asked, "What do you see here?"

She replied, "I see light. It is literally *all* light."

He turned to Stephanie and said, "What do you see here?"

She answered, "I see a distinct color light, and I see jewels and stones."

Malcolm said, "Father has intimacy with his new creation. He is always forming. He is always creating; you can share the intimacy with Him as a co-created one. Step inwards, outwards, and upwards. Defy physics!"

We asked, "How do we defy physics if it is relative and it is intimate?"

He replied, "When you are in Heaven, you can defy physics."

Stephanie replied, "I'm game. Help me to defy physics."

---

*Be in Heaven <u>and</u> on Earth
simultaneously
and you can defy physics.*

"That is where the intimacy is because you can simultaneously be on Earth and Heaven. You have heard this, you know this, and you have even had little exercises in it."

We asked, **"How do we do this day in and day out?"**

He replied, "Know that there is much intimacy with the Father in both realms. Draw from its light. Everything is light."

---

*Know that there is much intimacy
with the Father in both realms.
Draw from its light.
Everything is light.*

Stephanie responded, "Well, Father, I seek to stay in your light in this earthly realm and the heavenly one simultaneously, to move in it, and to walk in it."

Next, we were shown a mirror. Looking into the mirror, Stephanie said, "I see a line down the middle of me. One side of me is in Heaven, and the other side of me is on Earth. One foot is on Earth. One foot is in Heaven."

Malcolm asked, "How could you get off the Golden Path with one foot in Heaven?

"Stay here in these places. This is your rulership. Defy physics."

With that, he was gone.

———— ∞ ————

Chapter 6

What Are You Hiding?

One of the things we have discovered is that, by aligning your realms, a great deal of healing can occur to our realms as well as some interesting discoveries.

Many people struggle with disappointment and hope deferred. They have prayed and prayed and yet, no answer seems to come. Let me describe a couple of scenarios you may want to adapt to your own life and make discoveries about.

We were working with a client who, when querying her body realm, indicated a lack of trust in the Father because so many things had been prayed for, but the body had not received the answers. As a result, it was blaming God for not answering, but we know from Scripture that if we ask of the Father, we receive (see Matthew 7).

We decided to check with our client's soul realm to learn more. I had known that—particularly with healing—one can be in an atmosphere where a healing anointing is present; the person feels the touch of Heaven for healing, but the healing never manifests. We had discovered that the soul realm had become essentially a gatekeeper instead of a bridge. The healing anointing flowing from Heaven had come to the person's spirit, to the soul, to flow to the to the body where it was needed. However, because the soul was uncomfortable with the "feelings" it was experiencing, it had stopped the flow of healing, and so what was intended from Heaven never manifested in the person's body.

A similar thing had occurred with this young woman. As we were querying the woman's soul realm, I was impressed to ask if it had some things intended for her body stored somewhere. The soul confessed that it did; we could envision it walking over to a storage chest and opening the lid. Inside were all kinds of things, including healing anointings for certain things.

The soul apologized to the body realm for keeping these things locked away and not allowing them to go where they were intended. The soul then began to deliver the various things to her body realm.

The body realm realized it had blamed God for not coming through when the reality was that the soul was the culprit. As the hidden things were released into the young woman's life, hope was restored. Over time, the various things began to manifest in her life as they were originally intended.

I shared this experience with Dr. Rodich, who decided to check his own soul for things that had possibly been kept back. He made the discovery that several healing anointings had been held back. He began the process of recovery from the hidden things and began to feel an immediate improvement in his body. He understood the wisdom of not having all of them released at once so that his body realm could adapt.

We have found that by working with the various realms, healing from fragmentations and many other things that have impacted us along life's journey can come. We are just beginning to explore working with realms this way, but we are excited about the possibilities for wholeness.

I Thessalonians 5:23 has a whole new application. The verse reads,

> *Now may the God of peace Himself sanctify you completely; and may your whole spirit, soul, and body be preserved blameless at the coming of our Lord Jesus Christ.*

As our realms are aligned, the outworking of the sanctification process can be completed. As our realms are healed, we can be fully dedicated to the Father. We can walk out our scroll in our own lives. We will share in upcoming volumes as we learn more along these lines.

New Discoveries

As we explore the possibilities of aligning our realms, we also see tremendous opportunities for the healing of fragments or parts of the various parts of our being.

Because we are still discovering, we are not ready to publicize the methodologies yet, but we expect to do that sometime in the future. We have witnessed tremendous healing take place in people's lives as we explore the places where trauma has roots. We have found that we can heal traumas by working with the various realms. It is as much a timeline issue as it is about anything else.

———— ∞ ————

Chapter 7

What is Joy?

We had engaged Heaven, as we do weekly, to discover Heaven's instruction for Sandhills Ecclesia. On this occasion, Enoch asked, "What is Joy?"

David Porter, who was assisting me, saw Enoch and Paul come together and high-five one another. One of them remarked (speaking of David), "We have to train him."

David laughed and replied "Yes, you guys can train me. Okay—hold on again. What's going on? Elijah just showed up and they said, 'We're having a party!'"

Enoch, Paul, and Elijah said in unison, "Celebration is about joy. Joy is about celebration, but joy is not only about celebration. The scripture says that the joy of the Lord is your strength. Isn't that correct?"

David replied, "Yes, it is."

Enoch, Paul, and Elijah continued, "Joy is also an entity that Father wants his people to step into when there are worldly pressures and things in the world system.

There is a secret place called Joy.

"It is the entity you can step into. Remember the scripture that says, 'For the spirit of heaviness, put on the garment of praise.'[7] That is joy. Joy is also a fruit of the spirit. Is it a manifestation of the spirit? How do you feel when you experience joy?"

David replied, "When I experience joy, I feel light, exuberant, happy, and joyful."

They asked, "What else do you do?"

David replied, "I sing. There is a sense of excitement."

They asked, "How do you think joy affects your realms?"

David answered, "I have never thought about how joy affects my realms. I'll give it some thought."

The trio asked, "Does it strengthen your realms?"

---

[7] Isaiah 61:3

David replied, "I would say yes. The joy of the Lord *is* my strength."

The trio remarked, "Joy doesn't carry your strength, but joy carries His strength—His strength—the strength of the Father. What are some examples of expressions of joy?"

David answered, "Well, some people cry because they get so happy. Some people won't, and some people laugh."

The trio remarked, "Do you remember the scripture that says laughter is like medicine?[8] Joy brings healing."

The trio asked Stephanie (who was also assisting), "What do you think of when you think about joy?"

Stephanie replied, "I think about my encounter in Heaven that I had when I stepped in and heard, 'The joy of the Lord is your strength,' and it began raining—beautiful, good rain. Big drops of what I would say was living water. I was a little girl, and I was just dancing in the rain and spinning around and round, and I would throw my neck back and hold my mouth wide open and I would get the rain in my mouth.

"I turned, and suddenly, Jesus was standing there. He had his mouth full of water, and He just spit it out. We laughed and laughed, and then we danced in the rain. That's what joy is to me. I heard a voice say, 'You

---

[8] Proverbs 17:22

two look like you're having fun,' and I turned around. It was my daddy, who passed away when I was twelve, and then we danced. That's a joy story."

One of the trio replied, "Joy is light."

David remarked, "I've never heard that before. Oh, joy is light. Joy—light. Wow!"

Stephanie commented, "Light has multiple meanings in this. It makes you light as a feather and also has light."

One of the trio said, "Liberation, illumination; look deeper and deeper."

David said, "Okay, I see a portal. It's called Joy. As I step into the portal, my insides are vibrating.

"They asked me the question earlier, 'How does joy affect my realms?' Well, I'm sensing the frequency of my realms right now. I'm seeing my spirit, soul, and body in the sense that the frequencies of joy are flowing through me simultaneously."

Enoch queried, "Is this joy unspeakable full of glory, David?"

David remarked, "Wow. I feel the glory and sense the glory—Joy in the Glory, and there's Glory in the Joy. The assignment for Sunday is for us to instruct the people that they have not properly embraced the joy of the Lord. His Glory in joy and His joy in Glory shift their understanding. It shifts their position.

Stephanie remarked, "The people are to step into the portal. I ran into the portal, and it was like those cartoons you see—I was flying, and I was so light. I would hit a cloud and bounce off that cloud, and I'd go to another cloud, and I'd bounce off that cloud and then another cloud."

David commented, "I'm experiencing in my realms a vibration, but it's a good vibration. I'm sensing healing."

One of the trio said, "In His presence, there is fullness of joy, and in his right hand, there are pleasures forevermore.[9] So as you step into the entity—the portal of joy—you step into the Glory, which is His presence. Many have downplayed joy, not having the revelation of what the Father had originally intended and without understanding His true purpose. You rob yourself of His gift. Replace the word 'glory' with 'joy.' The lifter of my head is joy and strength. As the joy increases, the strength increases. It's the Glory *and* the joy, and He is joy. This is glory. Joy is His presence."

David remarked, "Joy! Okay, I need to expand my soul now."

Paul asked, "Is there Joy in communion?"

Stephanie remarked, "I was thinking of all the people we like to be around and communing with

---

[9] Psalm 16:11

them—that is one definition, and Paul just showed me that we can find the joy IN Communion that we take into ourselves."

David added, "You're asking me how joy affects others around you. When you carry joy, how does it affect others around you?

"It changes the environment. It changes it. I have experienced being joyful, and someone said to me, 'When you came in the room, I was feeling bad, but now I don't feel that.'"

Paul said, "Within you, as sons, because you carry the Spirit of the Father, you carry joy. On Sunday, bless the people with joy. Release joy, release the Father's joy."

―――― ∞ ――――

Section 2
Quantum Realms

Chapter 8
Advanced Sonship Technology

"Advanced Sonship Technology" is the name of the course Dr. Rodich taught in the Winter/Spring of 2024 for the AfterCare program of LifeSpring International Ministries. In this teaching, he unveiled many things and challenged us to embrace Heaven's technology related to sonship. The next few chapters are from this course. One of the class sessions is inserted here.

Dr. Robert Rodich

The goal of advanced sonship is to move on from the 10% to 100% functionality as sons and daughters of the Most High God and to wake up our inner cellular structure on the road to transfiguration and a much longer life.

We need to understand the role of water, nutrition, frequencies, and gemstones because they help clear the static and chaos in which we live and operate.

We need to change our thinking to address the 3-D Earth and conform and constrain the mindsets that feed the soul and keep us tied to the Tree of the Knowledge of Good and Evil. Expanding our thinking allows us to open invisible doors, see in the spirit, gain wisdom, use our anointing, and receive greater revelation, greater finances, supernatural transportation, authority, and dominion.

We need to see that these resources are already inside us because the fullness of the Godhead dwells in us bodily and because we are seated with Christ Jesus in heavenly places. We need to bring them to full activation and manifestation, as well as identify our potential and liberate it!

We need to realize that the Holy Spirit *is* limited by the level of our personal restraints. His gifts aren't enough if we reduce their power by 90%.

We need to understand that Satan has spoken a designed curse format over humanity to limit our thinking and creativity as those created in the very image of God. We must learn to break free from this substitute scroll. We must be ever mindful of the bigger picture to appreciate the value of Sonship.

Remember:

- God wasn't lonely and needed a family.
- We are very ancient and have memory in our spirit of our pre-Adamic existence.
- Each of us was designed in Father's heart, and therefore, we each have a purpose, a special design, a personality, and our personal gifts and abilities.
- We are here *on* assignment.

The fall of Adam is the reason we have no memory of our preexistence. That transgression:

- Inverted the operational principles of our being.
- Severed humanity from the operational principles of God's Kingdom.
- Interrupted the flow of resources.
- Created spiritual amnesia.

Adam's assignment was to dress out and keep the Garden of Eden (Genesis 2:15), yet we have little idea of its scope. This leaves the possibility that Adam's assignment was more comprehensive than we imagined.

When our Savior lived his sinless life, died on the cross as the sacrificial lamb, rose from the dead, and then ascended to Heaven, He became the only means of restoration for mankind.

Everything else is purposeful spiritual misdirection.

As we fully accept the price paid for our redemptive restoration, we may then begin the process of rediscovering Adam's assignment, discovering who we really are, and understanding our individual role in restoring the creation around us.

A critical point of realization is for us to line our thinking and processing up with Heaven's operational principles and culture.

If we don't change our thinking, we will be locked into soul dominance and religious behavior.

As the writer of Hebrews wrote:

The message God spoke to us in Christ, is the most life giving and dynamic influence in us, cutting like a surgeon's scalpel, sharper than a soldier's sword, piercing to the deepest core of human conscience, to the dividing of soul and spirit; ending the dominance of the sense realm and its neutralizing effect upon the human spirit. In this way, a person's spirit is freed to become the ruling influence again in the thoughts and intentions of their heart. (Hebrews 4:12) (THE MIRROR)

This chapter aims to provide a clearer picture of our challenges and what we must change to become fully functional sons of the Most High God.

We are naive if we think that our enemy lacks intelligence or technology. In fact, his plan has always been to render us completely ineffective and eventually eliminate us. His plan operates in both the seen and unseen, governed by principles that operate according to the 3-D Earth and the spirit realm.

To rise above the enemy's plan and its cosmic legalities, we need to know what steps are necessary to remove all restraints and understand the technologies positioned against us (Ephesians 6:12).

They...

- Have created legal restraints against the Body of Christ.
- Are masters of lies, deception, misdirection, and fake religious experiences.
- Are totally evil spiritual beings that can travel into multiple dimensions, gateways, and pathways.
- Are beings that do not need sleep.
- Have sophisticated research and development capabilities with destruction in mind.
- Have technologies that would blow our minds.
- Understand how to hack our realms via frequency warfare, and they can see how effective they are by our reaction and how it changes our frequency, sound, and color waves.
- Invented disease to keep our realms in chaos.
- Changed 432HZ music to 440HZ to mess with our realms and song.

- Are behind genetic food modification to throw our inner frequencies out of balance.
- They are behind putting fluoride in water to calcify our pineal gland, which helps us keep our organs in tune with Heaven's frequencies.
- Understand how to use the daily news to keep us under stress.
- Have become masters at creating an environment that keeps the human soul in charge.

Their goal is to keep humanity from becoming fully activated in Sonship.

Our Response

The weapons of our warfare are not carnal.[10]

We have...

- The potential of full restoration based on Jesus' finished work on the cross.
- The power of His blood—Pontius Pilate's words.[11]
- The indwelling presence of the Holy Spirit.[12]

---

[10] 2 Corinthians 10:4

[11] Matthew 27:24-25

[12] 1 Thessalonians 4:8

- God's living word.
- Prayer and worship.
- Gifts of the Holy Spirit.
- The ability to pray in tongues.
- Glory/Fire/River of Life.
- Angels.
- Cloud of witnesses.
- Seven spirits of God.
- The Courts of Heaven.
- Our anointing.
- Our words/faith.
- Mantles.
- Gateways.
- Actual weapons.
- Gemstones (frequencies).
- Harmonic resonance (on Earth as it is in Heaven).
- Quantum Emotional Realm.
- Communion.
- Mountain(s)/stars/government.
- Heavenly health clinics.
- Heavenly training classes.
- Heavenly mentors.
- Heaven's bank.
- Heaven's culture.

Foundational Truth:

We are designed to live on both Earth and Heaven simultaneously. Until this becomes as natural as breathing and eating, we will remain people stuck in the 10%.

- This is who we are (our identity).
- Do we live in this as our reality or talk about it?
- Do we practice this as our reality?
- Practice interacting, practice listening, practice being in Father's presence.

A New Heavenly Blueprint

We can ask Heaven for a new heavenly blueprint for something like a new cardiovascular system or heart. Then, we ask God to insert his creative light and blessing into it. Then, being filled with the Holy Spirit, we can fix ourselves our anointing with the different portions of the Holy Spirit, each covering the frequencies of the color spectrum.

Once it is combined, we can release it onto the heavenly blueprint and receive it into our soul, making it a multi-dimensional blueprint.

Once our blueprint
is multi-dimensional,
the blueprint is prepared
to manifest in the physical.

Our soul is the portal where the new heavenly blueprint is brought into this reality from the spiritual realm.

From our soul, we release it (via our words) to whoever or whatever the blueprint is meant for and watch as it manifests and miracles happen.

I had this idea to request a new Master Blueprint for our entire being. Let's request that. Speak out loud:

We request from Heaven a new Master Blueprint for our own and our Quantum emotions, a new Master Blueprint for our Spirit, a new Master Blueprint for our soul, and a new Master Blueprint for our body.

We now ask the Ancient of Days to insert his creative light and blessing into these Master Blueprints that we have requested.

We repent for any ungodliness within us, and we ask the Holy Spirit to fill us.

We mix all portions of ourselves, our light, and our anointing with the portions of the Holy Spirit and the Holy Spirit's light, each color of the spectrum, and release it into these new Master Blueprints.

We thank you for intermingling and combining, and now we release each of them onto our souls.

We receive the blueprints into our souls to become multidimensional Master Blueprints, and we release each Master Blueprint to its proper portion of our being, and by the power of His blood, the Holy Spirit, and the Ancient of Days fire within us.

We ask for the fire of the Ancient of Days to come and burn up any membranes or restrainers holding our beings out of place and out of order in Jesus' mighty name.

———— ∞ ————

Chapter 9

A New Design for the Human Body

Dr. Robert Rodich

Let's take a moment to focus on what our walk is. By now you should be having a peek at the bigger picture, which is to say, those who are following a true path of sonship are different.

> *See what great love the Father has lavished on us, that we should be called children of God! And that is what we are! The reason the world does not know us is that it did not know Him (1 John 3:1).*

We are, in fact, different—yet we are also authorized to deliver.

> *I will give you the keys of the Kingdom of Heaven; whatever you bind on Earth will be*

bound in Heaven, and whatever you loose on Earth will be loosed in Heaven. (Matthew 16:19)

The question for us is: how do we take what we are learning from the theoretical to that which is demonstratable?

Revisit what is proven:

- Know the Word.
- Define how the Holy Spirit's gifts work through you.
- Clean up your viewing screen (soul static).
- Do all from a foundation of intimacy and love.
- Learn to stretch yourself and the boundaries of what your mind can comprehend.
- We receive 2 billion bits of information per second, yet only 200 bits get to our understanding—that must change.
- Let your confidence (not pride or stubbornness) be established.
- Build heavenly and earthly relationships.
- Learn to work with angels.
- Change the world around you.
- Define your purpose and stay in your lane.
- Really overcome.
- Inner chaos and static.
- Eliminate fear from your life.
- Identify things that don't work.
- Beware of false timelines.

Learn to ask questions!

- What does Heaven say this should look like?
- How do we affect a proper change?
- What is the root of the problem?
- Are there legalities to be considered?

Discover new (old) things:

- Heavenly technology.
- Gateways.
- Resources.
- Revelation.
- How Heaven assists us.
- Our role in continued co-creation.
- Glory, fire, the River of Life.
- Your star and your mountain.
- The stones of fire.

Word from Fiorella Giordano[13]

I am hearing an unusual word today; I hear the Lord saying that He is breaking off the chemical and energetic bindings of delay in your body—every experience of delay encoded in your body, your DNA, your nervous system, and your immune system, on an energetic and chemical

---

[13] www.fiorellagiordano.io

level, so that your waking expectation is not to place your chronic symptoms into the framework of your reality, or to expect the familiar experience of dead-end cycles, but rather to reframe your body into a greater measure of wholeness.

The delay tax on your being is being removed, and you are shifting into a completely new economy of health. It is more than healing. It is a divine health care system that yields sustainable life. Father desires to awaken the full set of keys of dominion over the second language of your body, which is epigenetics.[14]

The first language is that of DNA.

- You now have the authority to open and close chemical expressions in your being.
- You may now link with time gateways that hold Heaven's record of how your body should operate.
- You may now tap into cycles of grace and life that bless your being.

---

[14] Definition: stable change in cellular function without changes to DNA sequences.

A New Design for the Human Body

Recently, I ordered a book from Amazon by Ian Clayton on the three gateways of man. When it arrived, I realized I had downloaded the material years ago when it was free online. However, as I looked at it, I heard the Holy Spirit say, "His depiction of your threefold nature is linear because you would understand it better. In reality, it is much different. Each part of your nature has its own energy signature—each with its own substance that overlays each other. Because each nature is of a different energy signature, each depends on clarity within each realm to exchange information and allow the flow of heavenly presence. This presence and information are passed on from one realm to the other via spiritual osmosis. That flow is hindered if any of the three fields are compromised."

Static and Filters

Each realm has its unique set of potential static and filters that can be implemented. For example, the spirit can have issues from our pre-Adamic existence or wounds that we have experienced in our earthly journey. For the soul, traumas and various abuses set up these blockages. For the body, the issue is two-fold. The first is all things of the physical realm, like illness and emotional wear and tear. The second is this: things that come through from the soul and spirit that leave memories in our cells, organs, and tissues. The Holy

Spirit reminded me that we have all been working to *bring our spirit forward and clean our soul yet* have neglected how all these things affect the human body.

Water

Statistics tell us that the human body is 60% water. Water is needed to hydrate our cells and tissues. but it does more than just that. Water can be programmed since it is crystalline in nature. This means it can be programmed from issues that come forward from our souls and spirit and respond in real time to what goes on around us. This includes daily stressors, warfare, and everything Heaven has for us. Water can then take this programming into our organs, cells, and tissues and leave the memory behind.

It is vital that we use the highest-quality water that can penetrate our cells (osmosis) to provide proper crystalline structure so we can process and release light, sound, and frequency. It is also vital that we remove ourselves from toxic environments that would negatively activate this process.

A New Organ

Here are some ideas to improve the quality of our water. Recently, scientists have called the network of fluid-filled cavities in our skin and tissues an actual organ (system). The term they use is INTERSTITIUM, which is a contiguous fluid-filled space existing between a structural barrier, such as a cell membrane or the skin, and internal structures, including organs, muscles, and the circulatory system.

Fluid-filled means water in these spaces can be programmed with sound and light. It also means that water can hold energy-creating vibrating particles (waves). Where could these energy-creating particles come from? The answer is our co-creative thoughts, as our thoughts line up with Heaven! The center of this energetic fusion release is in the Quantum Heart Realm.[15] Scripture says, **"As a man thinks in his heart, so is he."**[16]

At this point, you could say, "Okay, I get it; we can program our cells and organs to function better if we use better water and think more heavenly." Yet this is only part of the story. What if water and its place in our tissues were designed to make us actual instruments? Enter hydro-acoustics with love as the foundational cord.

We are designed to carry the sound of Heaven into our cells, then into our tissues and organs, so that when Heaven's song resonates with the songs of our realms, we become an instrument to release Heaven on Earth!

---

[15] Discussed in the next chapter.

[16] Proverbs 23:7

Nicola Tesla said, "Music (sound) shapes the invisible!"

Could there be streams of incomplete programming flowing through us and all around us (creation) waiting for us to be that instrument? Our body is also designed to arc with our star and arche.

If you grasp this, then all the distractions, chaos, and trauma make sense from a warfare point of view because our enemy knows exactly what we are to be. One day, we may have music that will activate us on cellular and tissue levels, for which I nominate Adina Horner.[17] Until then, we may practice activating these by singing in the spirit and singing the Word.

The 10 Virgins and the Bride

Note the following chart, which concerns three different groups of "saved people," all with different focuses and access points.

Matthew 25:1-4:

At that time the Kingdom of Heaven will be like ten virgins who took their lamps and went out to meet the bridegroom. ² Five of them were foolish and five were wise. ³ The foolish ones took their lamps but did not take any oil with them. ⁴ The

---

[17] See adinasmelodies.com.

wise ones, however, took oil in jars along with their lamps. (NIV)

Virgins

Foolish
- Self-centered
- Still sins
- Grace as an excuse
- Word as legalistic tool
- Brain centered

⬇

Wood, hay & stubble

Wise
- Old paradigm
- Spirit-filled
- 5-Fold Control
- Ministry focused

⬇

Go with Bride
(looking for an exit)

Bride/Body

Governing Son
- Governing on behalf of husband
- Living in Heaven & Earth
- Establishing Heaven on Earth

This is all about the Kingdom and those expecting to wait for the Groom's return. Two of the three groups get into the wedding festivities. However, only one group qualifies as "the Bride." Those who qualify as the Bride are those who, like the wise woman whose husband was gone and understood that her destiny and, therefore, reputation was the same as her husband's, did the work of her husband's vision just as if it were hers. This is exactly what those following after sonship do until the Lord returns.

———— ∞ ————

Chapter 10
Engaging with Quantum Realms

Dr. Robert Rodich

As we contemplate our walk as sons and daughters of the Most High, we need to look at forces and principles that would affect that walk. This is the case when we consider the category of quantum.

In general terms, quantum means the smallest observable part of something. For our purposes, rather than observing small particles, we will consider how small particles of essence can affect us and establish a base for God to resonate with us, which results in how we interact with that which is around us.

Specifically, we will look at **quantum entanglement,** which in simple terms is the observation of something that, when divided in two, will show an exact response in both parts regardless of the distance between the two parts **(referring to an**

experiment scientists did where blood from the same person was separated by hundreds of miles and when stimulated by an electrical charge they both reacted as if they were together).

In Matthew 6:9-13 we see, "Your will be done on Earth as it is in Heaven." If we resist the temptation to make this only spiritual, we could ask, "What would that really look like? The Lord's will—what specifically? In us? Around us? In matter? How do we get from the thought to reality?"

Most of us have been taught that things are either physical or spiritual. While this is true as far as it goes, science and revelation from Heaven show us that all realms and dimensions' design and operational principles also have mechanical aspects. The difficulty is that most people only know the operational principles on 3-D planet Earth, where the focus is on what is easy to observe.

What happens when we start to engage in other realms that do not fit our normal understanding? We may mistake something mechanical for something spiritual because the operations of that realm are different from what we are used to. So it is with quantum. Quantum is interesting because it has mechanical and spiritual applications and quickly moves.

For example, If something is planted inside of us **(a gift, a mantle, the Lord Jesus Himself, a seed of**

healing, or revelation) and the source of that something exists somewhere else, then any external stimuli in either place where that "something" is would instantaneously affect the other. Imagine the possibilities here—both good and bad.

Based on Colossians 1:27, **Christ is in us** if we are born from above, so with His essence in us and Him being in Heaven, we should expect quantum feedback based on quantum entanglement. The intensity of that quantum exchange can be increased or diminished based on the level of clarity and faith we walk in. This is a truth the enemy does not want us to comprehend, that truth being that we are so connected that we have all we need to change everything around us. We are quantumly connected with Yahweh, Heaven's culture, Heaven's provision, and God's very heart. Through quantum entanglement, the results of that connection can be instantaneous.

Imagine you do all the legal work, forgive everyone, get fully delivered, deal with trauma, and operate in faith—then you can operate in Quantum Realms. Those realms are body, soul, and spirit, as well as the Quantum Emotional, Quantum Heart, and Quantum Essence realms.

Each realm has its own operational focus and principles. Certainly, with Christ in us and because He (Jesus) is the blueprint of all creation, we should have an expectation to operate well in and with these realms—remember, we are connected!

Like most things we do in life, practice makes perfect. We must be confident that it is part of the "sonship" role to engage realms and spiritual categories. With that confidence in place, there is no better place to find out how to engage various realms than God's Word. God's Word gives us a historical view of what people saw and experienced on the 3-D side of Earth's reality. However, we are free to revisit those examples of history and observe what was happening on the spiritual side as those events took place. To do so would add tremendously to both our knowledge and experience base.

By now, the hope is that the majority of issues that could serve as filters, static, or blocks have been addressed by an individual. With a firm blueprint from God's Word that person may begin to engage the various realms. A possible aid in such an engagement is the use of topically designed gemstone-based medallions[18] that raise frequency potential to bring clarity to the person seeking to engage in the various realms.

In the beginning, each engagement should aim to identify the level of quantum material that person has within them. In most cases, this would be to activate that which is already present. However, I am sure the Lord would not be offended if we asked Him to enhance

---

[18] For more information, contact docrodich.com.

or increase that quantum material or essence. Another way to look at this is how much we need to expand to allow what is already in us to operate as it should.

As we have been learning, the area of the physical human heart is the point of convergence of our three personal realms: body, soul, and spirit. It is also the seat of the Quantum Heart Realm and where the flow of the Quantum Emotional and Quantum Essence realms interact with our person.

While we bring our spirit forward to create an inner synchronization and governmental balance, the electromagnetic field of the Quantum Heart Realm allows us to interact with both 3-D Earth design and the designs of all other realms, including spiritual realms.

What follows is a vital step that can be overlooked as we begin to engage various realms. While we have learned to tell the soul to stand down as a gatekeeper and take its rightful place in the release of Heaven's flow, we often forget that the final gatekeeper is our mind or intellect.

---

*The final gatekeeper
is our mind or intellect.*

If this part of our nature has not been brought into proper balance, it will thwart or even kick out what it does not understand.

Engaging the Quantum Heart Realm

As we do with our soul, we must learn to tell our mind to stand down and center our true seat of thinking in our Quantum Heart Realm (Proverbs 23:7). I recommend an exercise where we begin to scrutinize how we process our thinking, meaning to test to see if our first reaction to any situation is out of our mind or the flow of our heart.

Personally, I don't think any of us can successfully engage the various realms with accuracy and lasting results until we change the flow of the thinking process. Our Quantum Heart can understand the supernatural while our mind—our intellect—struggles. Start with everyday situations and then move into things more spiritual.

Pause a moment, call for your mind to stand down, and call the Quantum Heart Realm to come forward to dominance in your Quantum Realms.

Once a level of proficiency is established in the exercise of the Quantum Heart Realm, then the door is open to engage all other realms like the Quantum Essence and Quantum Emotional Realms.

The heart is the seat of our awareness and emits frequencies others can pick up on. For example, we can pick up on whether a person is good and safe to be around. Science has revealed that the heart sends out four times the frequencies to our brain than what our brain sends to our heart, indicating that our heart may well regulate the brain and not the other way around.

If a person has learned to interact with their scroll, the heart knows the future. The heart can sense good or bad before the brain picks it up. The heart knows the truth and can pick up on the intentions of others. It can also sense moods and dispositions in others with a range of up to 10 feet. This is because the heart sends out electromagnetic frequencies that are loaded with information. The Quantum Heart can read the thoughts of others as those thoughts are transferred between the brain and heart.

With proper awareness, the heart can sense other realms' electromagnetic fields and operations. The human heart puts out biophotons[19] of light, which may contain creative essence with the potential to be transferred to others. This is especially important when praying for healing in others.

Another application is that we are designed to synchronize our electromagnetic wave fields with others based on common purposes. This applies to marriages, the workplace, and those progressing in their walk of sonship. Certainly, this means we can send substances of positivity and blessing to others from the heart.

---

[19] Photons of light in the ultraviolet and low visible light range that are produced by a biological system. (Biophoton, 2024)

On a quantum level, the heart can be extended to sense the well-being of others for whom we have a concern. The obvious application is increased accuracy in our prayers.

The heart can tune into the presence of the Lord, angels, and Heaven's plan and flow for that person. This is also handy when we sense an attack. In this case, it is good to step back, take a deep breath, and reset the heart to find out what Heaven is saying in the matter.

The Quantum Heart field can be extended to discern the best energy attached to possibilities that may come our way, essentially sensing which one Heaven resonates with the most. This means we could use the same technology to see what is on our scroll and know how to move forward in a season or situation. This would include finding Heaven's timing for things like travel and vacations. As we grow and gain a burden for areas or countries, we may use this technology to find God's purpose for an area or country.

Finally, we should practice extending our Quantum Heart Realm into the heart of God, which is our place of safety these days.

Engaging the Quantum Emotional Realm

I would suggest the next step in what a person should engage is the Quantum Emotional Realm. This realm is under the instruction of the Ancient of Days. It is the first of the Quantum Realms that we were enlightened to.

While we all have aspects of emotions in each part of our being, the critical factor is the inspiration and source of our emotional flow. In and of ourselves, our emotions will always be self-centered and self-motivated. Contrast that to the emotional foundation that comes from the heart of our Creator, which He wishes to share with us.

Engage the Father's heart in such a way that He can "rewire" your emotional flow and be aware that this flow contains far more than proper emotions. His emotional realm establishes and creates perspective, understanding, and life and allows us to release life-giving substance to those in need. It may well be Quantum Emotions that allow us to speak to Quantum Essence so that Heaven's design could manifest on Earth. Certainly, this is a topic of engagement that we all should spend more time interacting with."

Rachael Testa, in her book *Engaging Your Imagination for Raising Godly Children*, gives this insight:

> I see The Ancient of Days as the whole encompassed Spirit of the Lord, the Godhead all together. The Lord told me the Ancient of Days is the Godhead in the Quantum Emotional Realm. Our emotions were defiled and separated from God at the fall, and they were turned

inward towards ourselves and into selfishness. The fall made our emotions about ourselves when God's emotions are supposed to drive us. We are to allow His emotions to flow out of us, which drives us to do His work in love for people.

What the Lord is saying is that the Ancient of Days rules over the Quantum Emotional Realm in an undefiled state, and when we align ourselves with the Heavenly Alignment process, we align ourselves with and in relationship with God. Then, we can access restored emotions and a restored soul and body. That is what Jesus did on the cross.

We align when we are restored and operating with a renewed mind. It's the state we were in before Adam's fall, and we can operate that way because of what Jesus did on the cross.[20]

Engaging the Quantum Essence Realm

At some point in our walk of sonship, we will be directed to establish a part of Heaven on Earth or have the invisible become visible. This is where Quantum Essence plays a role. Jeremy Friedman will discuss this realm much more later in this book.

---

[20] *Engaging Your Imagination for Raising Godly Children.* (Scroll Publishers, 2024)

Hebrews 11:1 gives us some insight into this realm: "the substance of things hoped for and evidence of things not seen." Wow, having evidence of something that does not exist before it is brought into existence!

As we all become more familiar with this realm, we need to establish that it is far more important than our next meal or the new car we hope will be in our driveway. Quantum Essence may well be what we will speak to anchor Heaven's designs into the fabric of the 3-D planet Earth.

As parents, we would never give the car keys to a 10-year-old, and our heavenly Father would not either. It will be fun to see how the Lord processes us all through to the point where we can speak to this creative substance and see things appear as a result. Until then, let's have fun learning the ropes of this realm so that we are ready when that time comes.

Remember: you are quantumly connected, so center your thinking and expand into the Quantum Realms. Be patient and start small. All you will ever need is already inside of you in the person of our Savior. Do a proper inventory and be honest with where you are at so that you can let Jesus manifest through you and be on point for each and every assignment you are given.

─────── ∞ ───────

Chapter 11
The Quantum Emotional Realm

The Quantum Emotional Realm is the realm we first learned of from the Quantum arena. This realm taps into the emotions of the Father and brings their reality into our lives. Many of us were led to believe that the Father was a stern taskmaster, simply waiting for us to make a mistake, commit a sin, or say the wrong thing so He could punish us. However, scripture paints a very different picture of the Father than we have been led to believe.

It does seem that our view of our heavenly Father can be greatly impacted by how our natural fathers treated us, whether they led by an example that was filled with love or an example of meanness, harshness, anger, or fear. When we have experienced poor examples of a father, we often need much healing to progress in our walk with Him.

Often, we give clues to our belief system by how we address Him. Do we address Him as Father, or do we see Him as God? This is not unlike how we speak of our Savior—is He Jesus to us, or is He Christ? Jesus is much more of a friendly expression than Christ, which is a title, not a name. God is the expression for the Creator, but not necessarily friendly.

If our father was absent, we may deal with a sense of orphanhood and abandonment. King David, although he apparently was an outcast from his natural father, learned to rely on Father God for his abilities and confidence. He took the time as a shepherd to learn many things that would help him later in life.

Multiple contributors' tips and thoughts about the Quantum Emotional Realm will appear sporadically throughout the remainder of this book.

———— ∞ ————

Chapter 12

The Quantum Heart Realm

Dr. Robert Rodich

With knowledge comes great responsibility. We are the generation that is destined to break through to full restoration.

We are the generation that is destined to break through to full restoration.

We say, "Restoration of all things," yet what does that mean? What does it look like?

Is it merely the removal of evil influences and corrupted designs, *or* is it more?

If the answer is more, then what *is* "more"?

Could "more" be the restoration to our ancient path(s) and our full restoration to interacting with and governing the realms and dimensions around us?

For too long, we have processed our questions and thoughts through the filter of what is "seen" around us. We have championed the pillars of our doctrines based on men's wisdom rather than God's breath. Our course should be that which draws from God's holy living text in which we realize that we are from old and, as such, we must rediscover our ancient paths. The truth of who we are and that we are a special creation in the very image of our Creator (Father) has been purposely kept from us.

We are the generation that will unlock these mysteries and start the events that will lead to our Lord's triumphant return.

The Questions:

- Who will pay the price?
- Who will allow the inner expansion necessary to be a fully new creation?
- Who will visit those ancient paths?
- Who will make room for the King of Glory?

Let's explore the realms vital to our exploration skills and co-creative assignments.

Six Realms

We now know of six realms, plus how we engage with light and our ancient paths.

Personal Realms

1. Body
2. Soul
3. Spirit

Quantum Realms

1. Quantum Emotional Realm
2. Quantum Heart Realm
3. Quantum Essence Realm

How we engage with heavenly light and ancient paths is in addition to these six realms. We could add Glory, Holy Fire, and the River of Life as engagement opportunities.

6 Realms of Sonship

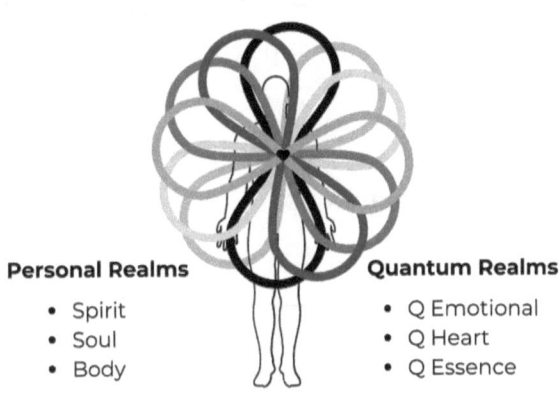

Personal Realms
- Spirit
- Soul
- Body

Quantum Realms
- Q Emotional
- Q Heart
- Q Essence

The term **quantum,** for our purposes, means:

Something inside of us that can resonate with its source in another location.

After being born from above, we had a great deal placed inside of us after the perfect design of our Savior, all He is, and all He accomplished.

The idea is that, over time, that which is above (Heaven-Yahweh) takes that imparted inner seed and resonates with it until it is fully developed. This is a process that takes place via prayer, worship, bible study, and heavenly engagements. Time and distance are not an issue as this process is *instantaneous* if properly engaged.

The goal is that we become the earthly instrument of Heaven. In Chapter 10, we learned about hydroacoustic resonance, even in our cells and tissues. The takeaway is that *we are designed to be tuned from Heaven and then release the results of that tuning into the 3-D Earth and any other dimensions we are called to.* This is how our co-creative purpose is brought into our reality.

"Christ in us, the hope of glory"[21] is **the deposit of our Savior's essence in us.**

---

[21] Colossians 1:27

- As a pattern, it defines our being and purpose and links us with Jesus in a very special way.
- It serves as a platform for harmonic resonance to promote growth and impart design.
- As we grow into the full stature of Christ, that essence permeates all six realms.
- It is corporate, yet we remain unique in our person.
- It means more Jesus while being yet more ourselves.
- This qualifies us for proper access to quantum entanglement with Jesus in all realms and dimensions.
- Jesus is the vine; we are the branches. We are the sap that flows, which is the quantum essence of creation and gives us access to Fire, Glory, the River of Life, heavenly light, and all realms.
- Jesus being the cornerstone means there is no other access point for humanity to access the fullness of creation around us—both the known creation and that which is yet to be discovered.
- Essence (creation material) must be allowed to sync with our realms to the point where our sight, realities, and understanding are upgraded to the point that our conscious reality reveals we can live in multiple realms simultaneously.
- Jesus' essence in us as a totally new creation changes our position and changes the created order within us.

Colossians 3 defines all this for us:

- We are raised with Him to seek those things from above.
- Our mind is to focus on things above, not things according to fallen Earth patterns.
- The old "person" is dead; we are now hidden in Christ Jesus—a greater birth process.
- We may now sever ties to the cycles of death, lies, and the Tree of the Knowledge of Good and Evil.
- The "new man" has a fresh blueprint that allows behavioral and emotional channels to be transformed by the Father's essence.
- This "new man" can now draw directly from the Father's heart, which is the highest possible source for our emotions and things such as kindness, humility, perseverance, and the like.
- The quantum baseline for all this is "love," the essence of which is imparted at our new birth.
- With love as a bond, we may build each other in various ways as we release the level of Quantum Essence we have attained.
- We also may now begin to demonstrate Heaven's culture and Kingdom dynamics.

Let me say—it is difficult to restore or release that which we know nothing of. For example:

Every geographical area has a Kingdom design, purpose, and a designed spark of life (essence). This is designed to send out a resonance awaiting a confirming resonance to be sent back. The fall of Adam changed this in many cases. Creation seeks that resonance to maintain balance, government, and purpose.

Everything of proper design originates in the heart of God. Our Savior has always been the point of release, and now He lives in us. His presence adds the holy fusion necessary to effect a change and also to maintain order.

In its malleable form, essence requires holy fusion to impart heavenly design initially or as something is being restored. Holy Spirit takes Father's design, Jesus' fusion, and releases sound and light waves so the design becomes a physical object.

The Quantum Heart Realm

Our proximity to Yahweh determines the scope of our focus and the range of the Quantum Heart's abilities. Other factors are intensity and our sphere of government.

The Quantum Heart is the central point of convergence of all our realms and the release point of our energetic field.

This is where information from the realms is processed, and we can release our field to scan dimensional possibilities and search for anomalies.

With the energy field of the Quantum Heart Realm, we can determine what Heaven may be saying as we scan the item of interest.

Let's be more specific:

Heaven has revealed that the location of the human heart is where all our realms converge; the heart is where all information is processed— "As a man thinks in his heart, so is he" (Proverbs 23:7). Other relevant scriptures are 1 Chronicles 2:8-9 and Romans 8:2.

Everything we experience, see, and ponder is processed in the heart. This is why it is paramount that we search our hearts daily. In fact, because the heart is the real processing center, it could also be called a birthing center.

The process is to extend the energy field of the Quantum Heart and scan the item of our intention or process what Heaven is sending our way. Consider it, then, when we feel we have the mind of the Lord, running it through our pineal gland, which converts it into bits of information that we may properly store in our brain.

It is not with the pineal gland that we see into the spirit realm, though—it is our Quantum Heart Realm.

Those who focus on the pineal gland inappropriately may actually be inviting a spirit in the family of divination to take control of this relatively simple process.

Once a matter has been properly processed and solidified in our understanding, we wait for God's timing and direction.

Father's influence is in our personal spirit (design), the Lord Jesus' in our soul (fire and essence), and Holy Spirit in our body (sound, light, frequency). The process of **releasing a heavenly blueprint** would go something like this:

Releasing a Heavenly Blueprint Process

- Call forward your Quantum Heart Realm.
- Bring forth the blueprint.
- Ask the Father to breathe on it.
- Call forth Jesus' holy fusion to combine with the fusion of your soul to activate the essence.
- As you speak it forth, call for the Holy Spirit to release the sound, light, and frequency necessary to manifest in 3-D Earth reality.

This is the true process of co-creation—true teamwork with our Creator to change what is around us.

Uses of the Quantum Heart Realm

Now, a bit more on what we can use the Quantum Heart Realm for—besides processing our own realm information, we may scan and process heavenly engagements, interactions with others, nature, geographical areas, political government, timelines, realms, and dimensions.

The Quantum Heart Realm is also linked with our other realms like the Quantum Emotional Realm and Quantum Essence Realm. We may use the resources from each realm to more effectively scan the information we are processing.

As we draw this topic to its close, let's brainstorm about ways to use the Quantum Heart Realm to process that which is around us:

Personal Realms	**Under the Dominion of:**
Spirit	Father
Soul	Jesus
Body	Holy Spirit
Quantum Realms	
Quantum Emotional Realm	Ancient of Days
Quantum Heart Realm	I AM
Quantum Essence Realm	El Elyon

Note

Concerning the thoughts and intents of the heart, these radiate approximately ten feet from you.

———— ∞ ————

Chapter 13
The Quantum Essence Realm

While Dr. Robert Rodich was teaching the class on Advanced Sonship Technology to some of our AfterCare students, a colleague of ours, Jeremy Friedman, was taught about a sixth realm that was previously unknown to us. He describes his journey in the next few chapters.

Jeremy Friedman

As I stepped into Heaven, I was taken into a place called the Waters of Purity. Instantly I could feel the presence of Holy Spirit rushing over me. My soul wrestled to find peace and stillness as I sat and soaked under the anointing. As I tried to quiet my soul to receive. I just wanted to think of all the chores and tasks that needed to be done because our souls are too often agenda-driven.

Without thinking, I proceeded to start praying through the process of aligning my realms. First, I submit my soul and body to my spirit's leadership. Then, I called my Quantum Emotional Realm and Quantum Heart Realm to align with my other three realms (spirit, soul, and body). As I did this, I could see in the spirit each realm personified and gathered together around the Father. Suddenly, a knowing came into my spirit about a sixth realm, or third Quantum Realm, called the Quantum Essence Realm.

I had knowledge that the Quantum Realms essentially were characteristics of the Father. Heaven impressed upon me that...

The Quantum Emotional Realm manifests within us God's thoughts or the mind of Christ.

The Quantum Heart Realm emulates the Father's heart.

The Quantum Essence Realm was new to me. I was impressed that it is like the Quantum Body Realm.

---
*The Quantum Essence Realm
is the Essence of the Father.*

Heaven said, "This realm is the Essence of the Father; this realm is submitted to El Elyon, which means "God (or Lord) Most High" in Hebrew.

The Father's essence is in all [created] things; it is malleable and palpable and *only responds to the voice of the sons of God. As we speak from a place of authority and sonship, we assert our priesthood over this realm, and creation responds.* I was brought to Romans 8 and the following scripture:

> *For the earnest expectation of the creation eagerly waits for the revealing of the sons of God. For the creation was subjected to futility, not willingly, but because of Him who subjected it in hope; because the creation itself also will be delivered from the bondage of corruption into the glorious liberty of the children of God. (Romans 8:19-21)*

As I pondered this, I was shown a vision of Jesus and the fig tree in Matthew 21:18-21:

> *[18] Early in the morning, as Jesus was on his way back to the city, He was hungry. [19] Seeing a fig tree by the road, He went up to it but found nothing on it except leaves. Then He said to it, 'May you never bear fruit again!' Immediately the tree withered.*

> [20] *When the disciples saw this, they were amazed. 'How did the fig tree wither so quickly?' they asked.*
>
> [21] *Jesus replied, 'Truly I tell you, if you have faith and do not doubt, not only can you do what was done to the fig tree, but also you can say to this mountain, 'Go, throw yourself into the sea,' and it will be done.* [22] *If you believe, you will receive whatever you ask for in prayer.' (NIV)*

In this instance, the fig tree responded to Jesus in authority as the Son of God, and—by way of the manifestation of the Father's Essence—the fig tree withered by the spoken word. This was creation responding to the sons, as referenced in Romans 8.

As we learn to partner with this realm and cooperate with the essence of the Father, we will see healings, miraculous happenings, situations, and places changed and redeemed. *Through the Quantum Essence Realm, we are changed into the likeness and image of God Most High, purified, and called back to our original nature as co-creators in Christ.*

The Father's Essence

As I engaged with Heaven another time, I saw my soul kneeling down and weeping in what appeared to be a dark room. As my soul wept, approaching him was a light that illuminated this room. As it walked near, the light appeared before my soul. It was Jesus. He asked, "Why are you downcast?"

Extending a hand to help my soul-man to his feet, with a burst of radiance and refreshing, I could feel this energy rush through my realms. It was the energy of the Glory. This was the Father's Essence or the Quantum Essence Realm.

Jesus had an army of angels with Him and many from the cloud of witnesses. He began to bring my mind back to the total solar eclipse that had recently occurred on April 8, 2024. I could see the moon completely covering the sun. Its darkness covered the Earth with its shadow. It was explained to me that when the Essence of the Father is removed, darkness appears on the face of the Earth.

Heaven said, "Living without the partnership of the Quantum Essence Realm can leave one feeling unfulfilled and bored. It is the Father's Essence that is in all things. It gives them their beauty, their color, and their radiance."

As I heard this, I could envision a cold grey world, like watching a black-and-white TV show. Suddenly, when the Quantum Essence Realm was introduced, the picture changed to vibrant colors, and the room felt full of excitement and life.

Peter appeared with Jesus and instructed me not to be foolhardy and neglect to work with the Quantum Essence Realm. He explained, "When we are in partnership with the Father's Essence, our expectation and faith to see Heaven move is elevated. It is a place from which we can draw upon the faith of the Father. It overrides the doubt and faithlessness that oftentimes dwell within our own souls.

Like it or not, doubt and unbelief try to replant and regrow themselves again and again like weeds in a garden. However, by tapping into the Father's essence, we draw upon His faith, power, and life-giving essence.

Jesus said, "Son, I know the cries of your heart this hour and this season. I know your deepest desires to see revival, to see yourself grow and walk in the greater manifestation of the gifts of the Holy Spirit and the power of God. I know that you have been praying for amplification of the anointing, no matter what the cost, yet a portion of that price to be paid is the understanding that, to do heavenly things, one must operate out of the realms of Heaven at all times. One must engage continuously. Understand that—despite what it looks like in the natural—when Heaven meets Earth, realities change."

Another voice spoke up at this point; it was John the Baptist. He explained, "This is the hour in which the Lord prepares the way. The signs have been written in the heavens. The shakings have been evident upon the earth. Have you had eyes to see and ears to hear? If not, let this be the hour of awakening your spirit man to these truths. Be a witness to the testimony of Jesus

Christ. Work with Heaven to see the immovable moved upon the earth."

As John spoke, I was reminded of a miracle I had seen a few weeks back. The Holy Spirit had come very powerfully into a church service a few Saturday nights ago. The gentleman preaching simply blew on me and I fell out in the spirit shaking, completely untouched by human hands.

John said, "This is the Quantum Essence, that miracle-working power—the Glory realms." I saw myself laid out at the altar, waking up, and getting off the floor. Nearby was a lady with rods and pins throughout her back and hips. She went up for prayer; she walked up to the altar with her cane, and she, too, was slain in the spirit. As the gentleman preaching prophesied and prayed over her, my seven-year-old daughter Genevieve grabbed my wife's hand and dragged her to the front in astonishment. This small child opened her eyes and was staring intently at this lady. She turned to my wife and said, "Mommy, is she really going to get up and not need her stick anymore?"

My wife responded, "Well, if you have faith that she will be healed, then YES, Jesus will heal her, and she won't need her cane anymore."

Genevieve sat in the front and waited for nearly an hour for the woman's spirit to return to her body and for her to get up off the floor. When she did, this lady was completely and miraculously healed! She walked out of the church without a cane or assistance that night.

John said, "Remember the instruction to expect to see the miraculous manifest.

"We must abandon our ideas and notions that prayer won't work or healing won't happen. We must forget the places in the past where prayers did not seem to be answered. We must thank the Father. We must learn to feel His emotions, and we must learn to operate out of His realms of Glory."

He continued, "The Essence of the Father is present to do the work. The saints on Earth are calling for things but not for the working of the wonders and miracles. Are you willing, son of God? Are you willing?"

Jesus said, "You have the knowledge and the power dwelling within. Be mindful to walk in it and step into it."

As He said this, I could see the Father standing before me. I stepped forward into Him by faith—into His essence and love. As I did this, I could feel the winds of Heaven blowing in and through me. In a vision, I saw the Father's hand outstretched with the whole earth held and cradled within His hand, and surrounding the planet were waves of Glory.

Father said, "My son, what you are learning is not new. It's just a puzzle piece that had been misplaced. You have learned how to commission your angels to use silver capture bags that release the Essence of the Father. You've learned how to align your realms, and you have learned about the Quantum Realms. This final piece ties it all together. *My Essence is in all people, all plants, all animals—every grain of sand on the seashore and all creation. My essence is the place that cries out to the deep places of your heart.* My essence is what provokes one to the heart cries of intercession and deeper intimacy. My Quantum Essence is in the heart of my sons and daughters. That makes one weep and cry for the things I weep for. Be in fellowship with me."

As the Father said this, He placed one hand on my head and one on my heart without speaking a word. I could feel his power coursing in and through me, rejuvenating my mind, rejuvenating my heart, and charging my body fully with essence.

As the engagement ended, I felt compelled to look up the definition and synonyms for the word "essence," and it came as no surprise to see the words "spirit," "lifeblood," "center," and "essential part" listed since His spirit is the lifeblood within all creation, the center of our existence, and a central part of our ability to operate within all the realms of sonship truly. Let us learn to work with the Quantum Essence Realm more intently as we engage all Heaven has for us to bring onto the Earth these days.

———— ∞ ————

Chapter 14
Working with Frequencies from the Quantum Essence Realm

Jeremy Friedman

As I engaged with Heaven one Saturday morning after a week-long battle with my health, I found it hard to press into the presence of God. My soul was weary, my thoughts were racing, my body was worn out, and I felt flustered.

I wondered, "Why am I experiencing such hardship?" I could feel my heart so burdened inside my chest and I asked the Father what was going on with me. I started questioning and wondering what the issue was. Was it side-effects from medications? Sleeplessness? Had I been striving too much?

Suddenly, the Father's voice broke through my consciousness though this process and said, "My son, tune to the flow of Heaven."

I took a breath, aligned my realms to get spirit first, and immediately saw waterfalls in Heaven. I pressed in for more and heard children laughing. Then I heard and saw a little boy drying a puppy who had just had a bath, flinging bubbles everywhere. Next, I could hear birds chirping and feel the warmth of the summer sunshine. The Father said, "These are a few of my favorite things."

As I kept pressing in, He sat me on his lap and applied slight pressure upon my back with his hands to calm me.

He said, "My son, the devil himself will appear to you, burdening you with business. Do not be burdened under Satan's yoke. Rather, be wise to his strategies and overcome them with heavenly resources."

As He said these things, He clapped his hands twice, and some attendants entered the room.

Looking around, I could see we were in the Throne Room. Before us stood three men in white: Mitchell, Malcolm, and Michael. Michell and Malcolm, I recognized from prior engagements. Michael introduced himself as a "Professor of Spiritual Sciences." These men brought with them a smart board that was wheeled into the room and a large old book. The bindings on it looked ancient, and the leather cover was worn and dusty. Across the front, in gold letters, it read, "The Power of Frequency."

The Power of Frequency

The Father said, "I believe it is time we unravel this mystery for him." Many in attendance chuckled as I looked bewildered.

Michael asked me. "What do you know about frequency?"

I said, "Well, I think I know a lot, but I have a feeling the little I know pales compared to what I am about to learn."

He said, "You are correct.

"Frequency is one of the most powerful things ever created."

I had many questions, and I thought about that for a second: frequency as part of creation.

And then God announced, 'Let there be light,' and light burst forth! (Genesis 1:3) (TPT)

---

*God used frequency
to speak all things into existence.*

Michael explained, "All creation has a frequency or a sound wave. Sound waves make vibrations. Much like there are positive and negative ions in the Earth's atmosphere that contribute to weather patterns such as storms and lightning, there are positive and negative frequencies that can dampen or empower the flow of the anointing and life in general."

Michael said, "Like ions affect a human body, so can frequencies. You have been taught about the Quantum Essence Realm and the Father's essence. This realm has a specific frequency.

The frequency brings with it a shift of atmosphere and a predetermined set of characteristics hospitable to the environment of faith necessary for creative miracles to occur.

I blinked my eyes a few times, trying to understand what I had just heard, and asked, "Can you simplify that for me a bit?"

Mitchell interrupted and said, "Look at it this way. What happens when you mix baking soda and vinegar?"

I replied, "You get a chemical reaction that causes it to fizz and bubble."

He said, "Exactly, so let me explain.

"When you insert frequency into a situation, it can affect it positively or negatively and have a reaction. For instance, if you have faith in something, you pray for it, and you see it manifest. You have just mixed your faith with hope and added frequency through prayer; the response is the manifestation. When the Father created all things, He spoke them into existence through frequency, and through the essence realm, through the Glory, they were birthed."

Michael said, "Now, let's take a negative example: an individual is fearful of something, or they worry—that is a dampening or negative frequency set that weighs one down. The enemy and his camp feed off these frequencies. These frequencies smell like rot and sewage; the enemy enjoys seeing humans trapped in them. They will start to feed on lies and torment their minds and thoughts once the door to negativity has been opened. What can result is akin to a full-fledged panic attack. These frequencies are powerful in the *wrong ways* and have long fed into violence, chaos, wars, and death upon the Earth."

Malcolm handed me a folder. Inside was a hologram pdf displayed amid the Throne Room. It was a teaching by Dr. Ron on frequencies, both positive and negative.

As we operate at higher frequencies, we will see things change and shift around us.

As we speak out these frequencies, we are prophesying life over our destiny and desire.

Michael said, "As you speak out these frequencies, be intentional. What you speak *will* manifest because you are a son of God."

> *What you speak will manifest because you are a son of God.*

I opened my mouth and declared, "I AM BLESSED AND HIGHLY FAVORED. I AM FILLED WITH THE JOY OF THE LORD; IT IS MY STRENGTH." As I declared these words, I could feel the frequencies shift through me and there was a buzz that gave my heart a lift. I felt the joy erupt through me.

Heaven said, "What you are feeling now is called vibration. Frequencies have a vibration, and the vibration is what shifts you *and* shifts reality around you. The vibrational frequencies of Heaven work with and through the Quantum Essence Realm to bring about great change."

Mitchell asked, "How are you understanding these things?"

I responded, "They are new, yet familiar."

"Great! Let's keep going," he said.

The Anti-Christ Frequency

Mitchell continued, "Be careful which frequencies you allow into your eye and ear gates. Frequencies open portals. Foul language and hateful speech open up portals of destruction and negative influence. Be diligent in governing these realms and keep those shut. Utilize the equipping of your angels with grey capture bags for added security in removing negative frequencies."

He continued, "Negative frequencies being added to negative frequencies is like throwing water on a grease fire: junk will spray everywhere, and the flames will become out of control. We are sharing these things with you because this is one of hell's most effective strategies on the Earth to date. In this age and generation, frequencies of disrespect, rebellion, dishonor, hatred, disharmony, fear, death, and disunity are intentionally force-fed to the masses because Satan is continually trying to enslave humanity since his days are running short. These are antichrist frequencies.

"The antichrist frequency is prevalent in today's society. This frequency is truly damaging to generational DNA. It keeps many in deep-rooted religious cycles and keeps them believing lies. It deprives the children of God of reaping their true rewards and beholding their inheritance by echoing the lies of religion and poverty. This frequency erupts in jealousy and envy over others' blessings, mocking and rejecting others' revelations and testimonies. Worse yet, you have pride and arrogance in the place of mercy and love.

The antichrist frequency tries to shut down the anointing and flow in the Body of Christ, rendering the Bride powerless and impotent to fulfill her call in the hour we are in.

"There is a need for the sons of God to arise and redeem the body and equip the Bride to take back her authority. The antichrist frequency needs to be extinguished at first sight so that doubt, hopelessness, and faithlessness do not prevail, resulting in the second death (spiritual death).

"As you learn to flow with the Quantum Essence Realm, living out of this realm of Glory is imperative. As you live in this place and carry it with you, speak out the frequencies of the Kingdom to those around you. Bless others. Do acts of loving kindness to and for them. Live by the fruit of the Spirit, for these are the chain-breaking frequencies.

"The fruit produced by the Holy Spirit within you is divine love in all its varied expressions:

- Joy that overflows,
- Peace that subdues,
- Patience that endures,
- Kindness in action,
- A life full of virtue,
- Faith that prevails,
- Gentleness of heart, and

- Strength of spirit.[22]

"Never set the law above these qualities, for they are meant to be limitless.

"The goodness of God flows through frequency, and as you bring quantum shifts to others' lives by using the power of frequency to deliver all creation, the Father's goodness will win souls and bring the lost back from the worship of Baal."

> *Or do you despise the riches of His goodness, forbearance, and longsuffering, not knowing that the goodness of God leads you to repentance? (Romans 2:4)*

The Father said, "This is wisdom for the ages, my son. Be careful to guard your tongue and let Holy Spirit be set as a seal upon your heart and your mouth.

As a son, you shall have the fruit of what you speak.

What words you sow shall be the harvest that you reap. Keep your speech unblemished and undefiled by godless, unfruitful mysticism and prophesy life over all things.

"Speak words of life and great value over your family, business affairs, faith, and homes. Speak words

---

[22] Galatians 5:22-23 (TPT)

of great value over your enemies and your adversaries. Judge them not with a scornful eye but look upon them with mercy and compassion, for their need is great. The hours will soon come where their reward shall be served to them."

As Father spoke, I nodded.

Mitchell said, "A final caution: those who are in leadership, those who are prophets, heads of households, families and homes—give ear, let these words be stored in your heart, bless and do not curse, build up and do not break down, sow seeds of mercy, not of scorn, for when you speak so, the Father's voice can be heard through you, and your adversary, the devil, has long used the antichrist frequency to turn the hearts of the masses against hearing the Father and knowing his goodness."

> *In fact, the mindset focused on the flesh fights God's plan and refuses to submit to his direction because it cannot! (Romans 8:7) (TPT)*

He continued, "Do not be the source of further burden to them but deliver them in love. Prophesy over their lives as if it was your own child stuck in the world and headed toward spiritual death, that they too may be saved and attend the Wedding Feast of the Lamb by your sides."

I asked, "Is there a process we should learn to deal with the negative frequencies?"

Malcolm said, "There is not a formal process needed like one might use when entering the courts, but rather being assertive, confident in God, and standing fully in authority knowing that as you speak, the frequencies of Heaven will overtake the negative frequencies and shift atmospheres.

The Process

"A few simple strategies, however, that may be beneficial for the modalities of personal advocacy, intercession, and working with others are as follows:

- One can call upon the tuning fork angels to retune their bodily frequencies to those of Heaven in the Court of Angels.
- Heaven's Healing Hospital has a Frequency Healing Center. You can enter into this place and ask for the Angels of Purity to cleanse and purify your DNA and generational lines from all negative and anti-Christ frequencies. Afterward, ask to be attuned or re-tuned to Heaven's frequencies.
- Practice on your own. Align your natural and Quantum Realms. Prophesy, open a portal and step into it.
- Finally, instruct the Glory to stand up and arise within you. Then, prophesy, open a portal and step through it.

I stopped, realigned my realms, instructed the Glory to stand up, and extended my hand forward. I opened my mouth and, as a son, said, "Portal of Joy, open up."

In the spirit, I could see a blue-white ring of fire swirling around a portal, and the light in the center looked like liquid metal. By faith, I stepped into it.

As I stepped inside, I felt very light, and it seemed like all the weight and heaviness I had been carrying just melted off my shoulders. I could see blueish-white fire all around, but not the kind that consumed.

I put a hand on my belly, then my heart, and said, "Portal of Peace, open up."

I could feel the instant vibrational shifts as my frequencies shifted out of the earthly frequencies of worry and angst and were replaced with Heaven's Joy and Peace.

The Father said, "Practice these things in all your affairs. The world is sick with sin. Many are looking for these keys in the world, but through the access points of new age teaching, candy-coated fortunes, and occult rituals, they shall never have the fruit that they need but will harvest the sap from the tree which they seek."

I asked, "Papa, do you mean they are harvesting death by choice?"

He looked at me, nodded, and wept uncontrollably as He wept over his lost sheep. I started to weep, and it seemed all of Heaven wept with us. He dried His eyes with one hand and said, "My beloved child, that is why you are being entrusted with these things at this hour. It is time to reclaim Kingdom truth and deliver the lost from the lies of independence, self-reliance, and selfishness."

> *Those who are motivated by the flesh only pursue what benefits themselves. But those who live by the impulses of the Holy Spirit are motivated to pursue spiritual realities. For the sense and reason of the flesh is death, but the mindset controlled by the Spirit finds life and peace. (Romans 8:5-6) (TPT)*

As the engagement ended, Mitchell handed me the leather-bound book, and by faith, I received it into my heart so that I could walk in the fullness of this newfound knowledge and revelation.

———— ∞ ————

Chapter 15
Dimensional Transformation

Jeremy Friedman

One morning, as I entered the Business Complex of Heaven to meet with my heavenly advisory team, we were joined by Moses, Elijah, Enoch, Abraham, and Noah. On the table before us was a substance that looked transparent in appearance and like a mixture of jelly and water. Its shape and consistency seemed to be like jelly but it moved and rippled like water.

Moses said, "Today, you need to learn about dimensional transformation and how it relates to delivering the creation."

The entire universe is standing on tiptoe, yearning to see the unveiling of God's glorious sons and daughters! [20] *For against its will the universe itself has had to endure the empty futility resulting from the consequences of human sin. But now, with eager expectation, [21] all creation longs for freedom from its slavery to decay and to experience with us the wonderful freedom coming to God's children. [22] To this day we are aware of the universal agony and groaning of creation, as if it were in the contractions of labor for childbirth. [23] And it's not just creation. We who have already experienced the firstfruits of the Spirit also inwardly groan as we passionately long to experience our full status as God's sons and daughters—including our physical bodies being transformed. (Romans 8:19-23) (TPT)*

Noah spoke and said the dimensions and all reality are changed and transformed by the spoken word and the response of the Quantum Essence Realm to the sons of God. The spoken word brings transformation, not just in one's own life, but this transformation has trans-dimensional impacts.

I felt like a fish out of water and glared at Noah like a deer in headlights. The men in white and angels giggled at my confusion.

Elijah spoke up, "Let me simplify this for you. Have you ever had a preconceived notion or thought about something?"

I nodded.

He said, "When that initial observation was proven incorrect, and you changed your perspective on the matter, did it have a continuous impact?"

I thought for a second and asked, "Do you mean like looking for the positives in a crummy situation?"

He said, "Correct. Simply put, when the sons of God speak the Word, live it, and walk out the Word in defiance of the circumstances surrounding them, it changes things. It doesn't only change things in the moment of time in which they live, but the entire pathway forward is shifted to resemble the new paradigm of the reality that they have shifted into."

Enoch remarked, "Think of someone who had been homeless and their life shipwrecked. Rather than confess poverty over their life and sit in their circumstances, they choose to speak the Word of God, confess his promises, live out of the Kingdom's surplus, and pull that provision down from Heaven in prayer and faith. The acts of prayer and faith shift their path, it shifts the trajectory of their lives and their generations. Essentially, these acts of walking out their faith break bondages and meet Heaven's desire to have the sons taste and see the Father's goodness. As a result, the individual's mindset shifts and they adapt a provision mindset, they embrace the spirit of wealth and the things that begin to manifest for them and their generations are the manifestations of the Father's limitless provision."

I said, "This scenario sounds vaguely familiar."

He smiled and responded, "Can you see how you have lived this out and how this path has shifted in your life?"

I nodded.

Moses spoke, "Continue to confess the Word of God in opposition to all you see upon the Earth; continue to prophesy provision, deliverance, and breakthrough. Continue to speak by the spirit to the Father's Essence in all things, calling into being their divine purposes according to the Father's will and you will see timelines shifted and transformed. Destinies will be realigned and altered for the Lord's purposes and the unfathomable will be made possible because all things *are* possible with God. Believe for it and as you walk it out, your angels will go forth before you to help bring it to pass. This is an act of blind faith and living with Hebrews 11 as a living part of your being. All things are possible when your faith is fully reliant on God and coupled with the expectation that it will manifest here and now."

As he spoke, I saw the blob on the table transform into a picnic basket full of delicacies. As this encounter concluded, Abraham said, "Faith is the substance of things hoped for and the evidence of the unseen."

As I meditated on what I learned, I put it into practice and coupled it with prophesying to open the portals of provision. I started declaring the opposite of certain situations I had been contending for God to move in. What I witnessed the remainder of the day was supernatural, to say the least. Business needs and financial breakthroughs were at the core of my personal concerns that morning. I started to speak life into and over those situations, speaking advancement, increase, and favor into them by faith, trusting what I had just learned would immediately manifest. To my pleasant surprise, it went far beyond my wildest expectations.

I challenge you this day to try this on your own. By faith, prophesy the dimensional shifts in your life and watch Heaven move on your behalf.

———— ∞ ————

Chapter 16
Quantum Realm Angels

Flavia Diaz

As I was aligning my realms with the Realm Angels and got to the quantum parts, I wondered if they also had Realm Angels. I made a note to ask the Help Desk that question.

At the Help Desk, I asked if someone could clarify whether the three Quantum Realms have Quantum Angels assigned to them, and a man in white named Jerry came forward.

Jerry answered, "Yes, there are angels assigned to your Quantum Realms. The Father is quite thorough in His work of creation; He doesn't leave anything to chance.

"These Quantum Angels are a bit different than the body, soul, and spirit angels. They are closer to the Father in that they bring—from within the Father—the things necessary for your quantum growth and development.

"These angels lived inside the Ancient of Days and were created specifically for each of His children's quantum parts. Each angel was created with a specific blueprint for that person's quantum parts.

"The Father also has Quantum Realm Angels that minister to Him, and He created you in His image and likeness."

I asked, "Does the Trinity or Godhead have Quantum Realm Angels that minister to them?"

Jerry replied, "Yes, they were created for that purpose, but they lived inside the Father and He brought them into existence. He loves His creation and all that has been created *lived inside the Father before He brought them out or created them out into existence.*

"This is the time for mankind and angels to co-labor in accomplishing Kingdom business. They are excited to work with you in creating Heaven on Earth, taking dominion until Messiah Yeshua returns to get His bride.

"Learn to work with all your angels and don't neglect them. Acknowledge them and request daily what they need for co-laboring.

"The Father is a very creative being as you already know, and He delights in making all things different. The Father is spirit, and His creative parts include His Quantum Emotional Realm, His Quantum Essence

Realm—which is His goodness and love, and His heart—which is where all His parts, essence, and emotional realms meet. He delights in creating creatures and beings that depict and/or have and demonstrate a part of His character and being. For instance, He made you.

"The Realm Angel He assigned to you fits you like a glove, tailored to you. The Father gave them blueprints to help you navigate and prosper in your blueprint and scroll.

"The more time you spend in the Quantum Realms of Heaven, the more you will develop your Quantum Essence, Emotions, and Heart to align to the Father's until you are one."

(When he said the "Quantum Realms of Heaven" I got the notion that my Quantum Realms are connected to the Quantum Realms of Heaven, which in turn are connected to the Father's and are from the Father).

He continued, "Why are you surprised that the Trinity has Quantum Angels that minister to their quantum parts? I know this is fantastical, and you'll not find this information in the scriptures, but didn't The Lord say to his disciples, 'I have much more to tell you, but you cannot bear it now?' But now is the time for the sons of God to shine with the Glory, Wisdom, Knowledge, and Understanding of the Spirit of God.

"Everything the Father creates, He tends to, and He assigns his angels and other living creatures to see to its care, growth, development, knowledge, and cooperation with the plans of the Father.

"It is not far-fetched that the Father, Holy Spirit, and Lord Jesus would have Realm Angels for their quantum parts, and—in the case of Lord Jesus—for His glorified body and soul as well."

I responded, "You mentioned that these angels lived inside the Ancient of Days and were different than other angels. In what way? Can you expand on that please?"

Jerry replied, "These angels were not in the imagination of the Father where He would speak and Lord Jesus would create them. No, these angels were in the very core of his being—in His heart. They were a combination of all He is, a convergence of His essence, emotions, creativity, love, goodness, wisdom, knowledge, understanding, strength, infinity, purity, holiness, justice, truth, and spirit. From all His attributes He made these angels. They have the special role of caring for His creations' quantum being.

"Develop your quantum parts and you will operate more like your Father in Heaven. These angels' jobs are to help you develop those quantum parts to become more like the Father. The Father is spirit and those who worship Him must worship Him in spirit and truth."

As he said that last part, in my mind I wondered, "Are the Quantum Realm and Spirit Realm different facets of the same reality?"

I decided to ask, "How does our spirit relate to or what is the role of our spirit in light of these Quantum Realms?"

Jerry replied, "The Quantum Realms are *in* your spirit. Develop them as you develop your spirit. You already have the tools."

Then he said, "That will be all for now."

I thanked him and he left.

———— ∞ ————

Chapter 17
Cleansing Our Realms & Heavenly Alignment

Dr. Robert Rodich

Adam's transgression made humanity and near creation vulnerable to hacking. This truth has only become understandable with the invention of computers. The possibility of spiritual hacking is something that the church rarely addresses.

Genesis 2:25 tells us that Adam and Even were naked yet had no shame. It seems plausible that they were covered with Glory which acted as a supernatural covering. Yet soon after, they hid, seeing that they were naked. What happened?

Their transgression removed their covering. Perhaps without a full understanding of the ramifications of their actions, they opened a massive door to the enemy and surrendered their directive of purpose.

Previously, they were connected to the Tree of Life and all the resources of Heaven. Their act of disobedience transferred their connections and abilities to another system—an evil system, very foreign to all they had known and with unknown consequences at that moment.

It didn't take long to find out what they had done. To begin with, they were created with their spirit forward; now, their spirit became inverted, trapped inside their body and soul. This created a vulnerability similar to a computer system with a "backdoor" for hackers to enter.

The security of mankind's energy field was compromised, DNA was affected, emotional abilities became vulnerable, and mankind's lifespan was altered.

The wonderful news is that those who have accepted Jesus Christ as Lord and Savior have the opportunity to reverse the effects of the fall.[23]

Today, we will look at how we can evaluate the damage and make a plan for full restoration.

---

[23] John 3:16

Understanding Our Realms:
Spirit, Soul, and Body

As I wrote in my book *Moving Toward Sonship*,[24] each part of our being has its own voice, mind, will, and emotional aspects that must be synchronized so that we may know what our personal spirit has been up to all along. Our natural mind must be in touch with our spirit. This is necessary as we transition to demonstrable sonship.

---

*The goal is union within
and then union with the Lord.*

In our greater group of those moving in sonship, we often hear stories about people preaching or doing miracles in various places around the Earth, yet they often tell us they didn't know they did such a thing. How is this possible? The answer is that we need a greater synchronization between spirit, soul, and body so we can be aware of the exploits of the new creation we are in Christ Jesus.

In my recent teaching series on Advanced Sonship Technology, I listed 13 categories of spiritual resistance we face.[25] The purpose of this resistance is to:

---

[24] Available from DocRodich.com.

[25] See Chapter 9.

- Keep us spiritually ineffective by blocking inner union and union with Yahweh.
- Get us to agree with the enemy so he can use our authority.
- Use our DNA for nefarious purposes.
- Get us on false timelines.
- Keep us bound emotionally.
- Minimize our faith.

I also listed 27 categories of items that really are Heaven's technology.[26] Each can be used to establish the culture of the Kingdom and Heaven's culture deeply within us and then spread to those around us and beyond.

Removing filters and static helps us benefit from the frequency spectrums the Lord uses to bless and tune us to His being. Also of great value is cleansing our DNA.

We have established that sound, light, and frequencies are universal delivery systems. We can be hacked because the fall opened us up to dark frequencies that were never meant to be a part of our nature. By eliminating all the residue from our old nature, we position ourselves to benefit from the higher forms of sound, light, and frequency we were designed to benefit from.

---

[26] Again, see Chapter 9.

The gemstone medallions I make are also of great value, especially in the frequency department. Here is how they work:

- They block about 70% of EMFs (electro-magnetic frequencies).
- They are specially made to give energy.
- They are made to clarify frequencies that affect our heart (which is the point of convergence for our three-part nature).
- The Ephod and Mazzaroth medallions actually clarify spiritual static.

We are *positionally restored* at salvation, and we work it out as we identify areas of need. We move toward the image of our Savior as our perfect blueprint for life and godliness.

---

*We are then in a position
to release Heaven on Earth
as the Lord directs each individual.*

The assessments I perform and medallions I create are part of a bigger picture of heavenly technology that includes the heavenly court system, Heaven's clinics, the Library of Revelation, and more.

In his book about bringing our spirit forward,[27] Dr. Ron equips us to reverse the inversion of body, soul, and spirit that resulted from the fall. As we identify and remove the filters and static, we are in a greater position to *"keep our spirit forward." This needs to be our permanent position!*

The goal is for us to be the open Heaven. For us to be the revival. To move from the 10% functionality that the majority of the church is locked into and move above the 70% level where we begin doing the greater works and works of restoration.

───── ∞ ─────

---

[27] *Living Spirit Forward: Second Edition.* (LifeSpring Publishing, 2024)

Section 3

Practicing a Lifestyle

Chapter 18
Separating from the Tree of the Knowledge of Good & Evil

Every person ever born has had to contend from one degree or another with the Tree of the Knowledge of Good and Evil. It was the focus of Adam and Eve's downfall in the Garden of Evil. We must unplug from that information source to embrace true sonship. We are living in a microwave society. We have become so accustomed to having things available in an instant. We have fast food available, instant breakfast, the notorious TV dinner, and the microwave oven. How many have stood at the microwave and wanted it to hurry up?

Have you ever seen the drawing of the little girl holding a small teddy bear, and Jesus had His hand out to her, wanting her to give it to Him? What she did not know was He had a larger and better teddy bear behind Him. She was under the illusion that she could not afford to give up her little teddy bear. The Tree of the Knowledge of Good and Evil often presents us with illusions and we end up disillusioned as a result.

---

*Remember,
you cannot be disillusioned
unless you are under
an illusion of some sort.*

The enemy will create an illusion that the Father will not care for you. Rather, you will find yourself living in the woods or under a bridge as a homeless person. That is typically an illusion that has no basis in truth or faith.

Some of us have gone through horrific things in our lives and we actually need to apologize to our soul and body for what we put them through.

Soul, I apologize to you for what you went through—the trauma of it. I apologize to you that we went through hard times. Will you forgive me, please?

Do similarly with your body if you need to.

At this point, Stephanie saw the little girl with the teddy bear and realized it depicted her. Once she realized that, she asked her angel to remove the Tree of the Knowledge of Good and Evil from her life. Her body took two steps toward that tree and said, "Are you sure?"

She replied to her body, "I am sure it is an illusion, and what we have instead of that is so much greater. I promise."

She asked the angel to show her body the Tree of Life and asked her to open the garden.

Stephanie remarked, "I want that little girl to come out of that other tree (the Tree of the Knowledge of Good and Evil), to step out of that tree because what this other tree has is much greater."

She watched as the angel took her out of the first tree, and she watched the tree disintegrate. Then, the little girl stepped into the Tree of Life. Immediately, patterns were visible, and the fruit was very different.

She said, "Body, this is where we belong. It contains everything we need."

Stephanie realized that the place where that first tree stood was like a timeline. She requested,

Angel, destroy that timeline and every residue, every technology, every spiritual debris. Destroy it and burn it.

I repent for every trade knowingly made with the Tree of the Knowledge of Good and Evil.

I repent for being enticed by it, wanting its fruit, for becoming a part of it—for that agreement, for walking hand in hand with that entity. I ask Jesus to cover it. I forgive, bless, and release myself.

Stephanie remarked, "I've been asking Wisdom—what is the story's moral?"

Wisdom replied, "This is for the people. Of course, there is life and life more abundantly. This is trust at its finest. This is a constructive trust.[28] The Tree of Life is part of your trust fund."

Stephanie was about to ask her body how it was doing, but it quieted her because it was worshiping. She watched as the feet of her body realm took root.

The backstory on why Stephanie had to apologize occurred many years ago. Her late husband, who was an alcoholic, had abused their finances, resulting in their eviction from their home. She was a new mom with two young daughters.

Her body was traumatized by the eviction because it had a lot of work to do in a short period of time. She also cared for the babies and all that goes with it. Essentially, her body went on overload and was never compensated for it. Therefore, the apology helps her body move forward. Many of you have had similar things happen to your body or soul. Many times, we place too much on our various realms, so it begins to shut down in areas. Your soul may not trust your spirit, or your body may not trust your soul. You need to query

---

[28] Find out more about constructive trusts in my book, *Dealing with Trusts and Consequential Liens from the Courts of Heaven*. (LifeSpring Publishing, 2022)

your realms and bring resolve to any challenges they are dealing with.

———— ∞ ————

Chapter 19

The Three Books

This engagement found us in a huge library with books everywhere—not just on shelves along the wall, but also on the floor. Stephanie noticed a short stack with three books. She felt drawn to it and saw that they were ancient books. The book's title on top was *The Book of Treason*; the smaller one underneath was entitled *Opulence*. It was an old book tied together with a cord. Finally, the third book was titled *Time Travel*.

A desk was nearby, so Stephanie placed the books on it and sat down to read. As she sat down, her Realm Angel for her body appeared. He pointed to the book Opulence. Opulence is wealth, affluence, abundance, or extravagance. She picked it up and opened the first chapter, entitled "Mind Control," with the subtitle "Efficiencies of Controlling the Mind."

Stephanie wondered why her Body Realm Angel assisted us this time rather than her Soul Realm Angel.

The Body Realm Angel explained that our body has a mind and a spiritual nervous system. Continuing to look at the first chapter, she saw an outline:

> A. *"Lean not into your own understanding, but in all your ways acknowledge Him," (Proverbs 3:5).* Stephanie immediately verbalized that she chose to do that with all of the minds of her spiritual soul AND body. Next was:
>
> B. *Train.* Meaning—to train with the Scripture: *"Out of the abundance of the heart, the mouth speaks," (Matthew 12:24).* And then:
>
> C. *"Beloved, above all things, walk in the way of His word."*

That was the end of that portion of the chapter.

Her Body Angel explained, "There is opulence in the brain function of the body realm that is very significant and distinct and plays a part in what is represented as the other two books." He closed by saying, "I give you ease."

She then noticed writing in red on the bottom of the page, which said, "I'm the way, the truth, and the life. No man comes to the Father except through me" *(John 14:6).*

Her Body Realm Angel asked, "Do you think that the body realm *mind* could comprehend this?"

Stephanie replied, "No; I would say that my body knows that it's going to return to the dust when it dies.

I guess I never asked that question. What will happen to this body if I don't die, If I end up walking like Enoch, or if Jesus comes back before I die? I know we get a new body. I get that, right? The question is, 'Does my body mind believe and understand the scripture that Jesus had said earlier?'— I am unsure where you helped me because you're my Body Realm Angel."

I asked if a commission for her angel was in order.

As I asked, Stephanie saw him pick up the words printed in red from off the page. He said, "Have the mind believe."

Stephanie began a commissioning:

I commission you to help take Jesus's words to the mind of my Body Realm; the words that state that Jesus is indeed 'the way, the truth, and the life and that no one comes to the Father except through Him.'

As she spoke, the angel fed Jesus words to what we think of as the body's circulatory system.

Stephanie prayed:

I want that word to be activated in my Body Realm system.

Stephanie remarked, "Somehow, I know this has to do with time travel, doesn't it? At some point, this is about our body being able to travel. It has to have a complete understanding, too, but it is a part of the system as a whole. That's why you have us working in unity and harmony with one another, with each realm."

The Body Realm Angel replied, "Indeed. You *will* walk on water."

Stephanie governed,

I speak to my Body Realm Angel that we will indeed walk on water. Angel, I commission you to bring these words of life from the Father, from Jesus, from His Word, and begin to nourish the Body Realm with that word.

She could immediately see the Tree of the Knowledge of Good and Evil on the front of the book.

The Body Realm Angel said, "This is the truth about the separation and the garden. It was indeed treason, and it was treason on all parts—not just on the part of the snake."

He asked, "Are you indeed trans-dimensional?"

Stephanie replied, "We are."

He remarked, "That was lost in the garden."

Our ability to be trans-dimensional was lost in the garden.

The Body Realm Angel asked, "Did not all three realms participate in the treason?"

Stephanie replied, "I saw Adam and Eve eating the fruit, and all three realms committed treason."

[Treason is from the Latin word *treisoun,* which meant to "hand over."]

The Body Realm Angel asked, "Do you want to be disconnected from the tree?"

Stephanie answered, "Yes, we do."

The Body Realm Angel instructed, "Repent for the treason to restore the body, to restore the soul, to restore the mind."

Stephanie noted, "I'm curious why you used the word 'mind'?"

The Body Realm Angel replied, "Because the mind of the body *is being restored.* "

Stephanie added, "I have a knowing that we also have to restore the soul mind."

Father, I ask you to return to that time as you are not bound by time. I would like to repent on behalf of Adam and Eve for the treason of their body, their soul, and their mind—the treason that was done in the garden from all three realms, acting in agreement with one another and in agreement with darkness and in attaching themselves (and all of humanity) to the Tree of the Knowledge of Good and Evil. Because of what you, Jesus, did at the very foundations of the world, Jesus, where you were slain before the foundations of the world, I would like for that blood to be applied here. I forgive them, bless them, and release them in the name of Jesus and all that came after, all the way to eternity. Father, we ask that you forgive us of all the treason we willfully, mindfully, and soulfully have done.

I ask for the amendment 'As If It Never Were,' a timeline reestablished for Your Kingdom purposes, the mind and body fully disconnected from the treasonous Tree of the Knowledge of Good and Evil, and all of the spiritual debris, essences, and residues left from being connected to that tree burned, swept up, and given to Jesus.

Thank you, Father.

I would like the mind of our soul realm to be disconnected from that tree, with all of its residues, essences, and spiritual debris swept up and burned in Jesus' name, and a disconnect from it to be given to our spirit man.

Before her prayer, Stephanie could see Adam and Eve standing in the distance, holding hands. As she was speaking, she watched Adam and Eve both take a step forward and turn to face one another, and she saw each of their three realms, which had been separate, come together into one being. She saw what was Adam's Body Realm, and then the Soul Realm came alive and stepped right into him and then the spirit stepped right into him—he is now one in full. Stephanie saw the same thing happen with Eve. "I recognize they're in a different dimension. They're here, but they're there. That's why they're not talking to me, but I'm watching what's happening to them."

She commented to the angel, "I would like to hand you this book, the *Treason* book, and for you to take it where it needs to go—that it not be here anymore, not present here anymore. I feel like I'm supposed to give it to you, angel."

The Body Realm Angel replied, "I work in all dimensions."

Stephanie then pulled the *Time Travel* book close to her but noticed a sticky note on the cover that said, "Do not open until...," and it had a blank date.

Stephanie asked, "Was the purpose of this Realm Angel to indeed prepare the body?"

The Body Realm Angel replied, "The things of this world need not weigh it down, but of other things to come. His righteousness strengthens the members."

Stephanie prayed:

Father, may we ask for the bonds of strength for our members to be placed in all of our realms, in time and out of time, and in every age and dimension.

The Body Realm Angel remarked, "Baby steps, Stephanie. Baby steps."

Stephanie then returned to her original position, looking around the library room. The stool where she originally saw the three books was still present, but now only two books were on it.

———— ∞ ————

Chapter 20
It's a Season of Portals

Father said to David,[29] "This is the season of portals—portals being revealed, experienced, and manifested. This is what the scripture means, 'The Earth is moaning and groaning and waiting for the manifestation of the sons of God.'[30]

"Your *eyes* are portal. *You* are a portal. *Everything about you* is a portal: your *eyes*, your *hearing*, your *hands* are portals. As you touch, you open portals. As you touch, you extend. You create portals by touch. Your *feet* are portals, your *words* are portals. They are life or they can be death.

"As you operate in your sonship, you also simultaneously operate as a Kingdom Ambassador, as a Kingdom initiator, as a Kingdom manifestation of the

---

[29] David Porter, who often joins in our engagements with Heaven.

[30] Romans 8:19-22

extension of your Father because you carry the very DNA of your Father.

"Walk, live, manifest, and create portals. You will see in this hour that there will be many who will experience transporting from one place to another, from one region to another, and from one time zone to another. You will also experience new portals—new portals that you have not yet understood or heard of, for Heaven has unlocked—the Father has unlocked and given you keys, maps, and map rooms. These were not only for angels, but this is for you as a son so that you can navigate and commission your angels to use the maps and the map keys that you have been given.

"Remember, you are to co-labor with them and you are to operate with them, not just commission them. You will also receive revelation so that when you commission them, you will have a greater understanding of their assignment as you commissioned them. This is the call; this is the shift to properly use portals. The purpose of the portals is to mature the sons to arise and take dominion.

"As I've ordained before the foundation of the world, you are My assignment because I created you to be My extension, My eyes, My ears, My hands, My feet, My heart. You are My body. As sons, as sons, as *true* sons, stand in your sonship, operate in your identity. As you open your mouth, I have already promised you that I will speak through you in that same hour. You, many times, will not know what to say, but you will sense the unction or the flow or the receptive door and entry into the portal. The portals, as they open, will beckon you. You'll be drawn to them; you'll be pulled in because they are aware of your position. They are alive. **They are entities.**

"There are many, many, many, many, many, many, many, many, many levels and dimensions and depths in glory. As there are heights in glory, there are depths in glory. As there are heights and depths in glory, there are widths and lengths in glory, for this is part of what I have called the body to do—to rule and reign. The kingdom of darkness already knows that you have access to them.

"Take your place, take your place, take your place," Father concluded.

David remarked, "This has probably been happening before, but I wasn't cognizant of it. The words I just received were penetrating. I wasn't just listening; the words were going inside of my being. This was a brand-new experience. I know the scripture says, 'Death and life is in the power of the tongue, and they that don't love it eat the fruit thereof.'[31]

"All of a sudden, I'm surrounded by portals. There's one over here to the right. I will step in. When I stepped

---

[31] Proverbs 18:21

in and I asked, 'Where am I?', I heard, 'You're in the future.'"

Paul, the apostle, appeared and explained to David, "This is the portal that I experienced. Become comfortable with the vibration and the frequencies of this portal. You will experience and see things that you will not be able to share until the Father releases you. This is one of many portals that will be open to the body of Christ. God has hand-selected many to be transported. You all have been taught to commission and to pray and to use the phrase, 'in time and out of time, back to the hand of the Father and to infinity'—these are the portals that you created. Every time you speak those words, then step out, step in, step out, step in—it is just that accessible.

"When you stepped into the Library of Revelation, you saw the books. When you stepped into the vault of LifeSpring, into this room that was in the library, you were stepping into the future. You were stepping into the mind of the Father. You were stepping into the blueprint that is out of time or that is in the future of LifeSpring.

"When I said, 'Whether in the body or out of the body, I did not know,' I had been released and I had stepped into this portal and portals like it.

"In my day, when I was alive on the Earth, there were many things I could not share because those who I was addressing could not perceive or understand—

now this is the season. Do you really understand? It is important that you understand the gravity of what is before you, the weightiness. This is not just a weight but it is *a responsibility,* and it is a commissioning from Heaven, from our Father. The Earth has been waiting for centuries. I understand you are processing, David; you are processing what you are feeling, how these things and how these portals work and this is impacting your realms."

David replied, "I don't have a place to put it, but I extended my soul earlier, and now I'm at peace."

Paul answered, "This is how the Ecclesia must be trained and instructed because there will be an increasing momentum of revelation that is being released because the Ecclesia has positioned itself to co-labor and to live from Heaven's dimensions.

"Ron already knows and is very familiar with these portals and dimensions, but he has stewarded this revelation well, and the Father is pleased. He has been tested over these last few years to release each revelation at its proper time.

"Now, you are learning how to steward. Stephanie is learning how to steward. Adina will learn how to steward, and those called alongside and those that will move to Sandhills shall be as a launching pad.

"What do you see, David?"

David replied, "I see Cape Canaveral. I see the place where the rockets are launched from."

Paul remarked, "That's what you are, that's what Ron is, that is what Stephanie is. Each of you is a portal, but you are also likened to a launching pad for the release of the flow of revelation.

"When you saw the portal in Eden last night, you saw the water coming and the portal coming down—the water coming down as a portal and then flowing out of the garden. That is how the revelations will be released and are being released even now. Do you feel the weight, the gravity of this glory that we're in?"

David replied, "I do, Paul. I do."

Enoch appeared and said, "Now you understand. Your understanding is becoming increasingly fruitful. You have had wonderful years of what it was like to walk with God. I learned to walk in revelations, but I also learned how to walk through portals. Stephanie has experienced that. She has seen me. Hi, Stephanie."

Stephanie replied, "Hi, Enoch."

Enoch asked, "Want some pie?"

Stephanie laughed and responded, "Yes. Blueberry, right?"

Enoch replied, "You got it, my sister. We eat a lot of pie here. I love pie. We have been waiting and waiting and waiting to fellowship and interact with you—with

God's creation, God's sons. Now we are excited. We wait with great anticipation to interact and co-labor with you and that you will experience what real life is—*to live in Heaven, while on Earth.*

Real life is to live in Heaven, while on Earth.

"As you now know, the real world is the invisible. Cloaks have been erected. Shields have been erected and they have been erected to protect what you are receiving. Angels have been assigned to release frequency jammers so that these revelations will be protected and properly stewarded by the sons of God. I have to go now."

In closing, David remarked, "That was fun!"

——— ∞ ———

Chapter 21
Ordering, Conquering, & Governing

My Executive Assistant and I had engaged Heaven and were given instruction concerning how our steps are ordered of the Father.

Not only do we have angels assigned to us and our businesses, but we can also learn to co-labor with them in order to see things accomplished in our lives, business, families, etc. Not only can we co-labor with them, we can also give them instructions concerning certain tasks. Psalm 103:20 tells us that they hearken to the voice of the *dabar*. *Dabar* is a Hebrew word found over a thousand times in the Old Testament. It has multiple meanings. A *dabar* could be a spoken matter, a book, a business, a case, a commandment, a communication, counsel, a decree, a deed, glory, judgment, message, oracle, a word or a work. It has far more possibilities than our typical translations limit us to. This verse tells us that angels hearken—give heed to the Father's business, His judgments, His decrees, His counsel, even the voice of His Glory! For us to instruct them to carry out the instructions of the Father is not outside of our purview.

Even though we may have been commissioning our angels to order our steps, we must also agree with the work angels do in the process.

Much has been said and taught about the Seven Mountains of Culture in the Body of Christ. We, as sons of God, are to dominate these various mountains. If our instruction is to establish a coffee shop, we should insist on becoming the very best coffee shop around and one that dominates its particular mountain. Since the desire to establish the coffee shop is in our heart, Psalm 37:4-6, the psalmist wrote:

> *[4] Take delight in the LORD, and He will give you **your heart's desires**. [5] Commit everything you do to the LORD. Trust Him, and He will help you. [6] He will make your innocence radiate like the dawn, and the justice of your cause will shine like the noonday sun. (NLT) (Emphasis added)*

Our responsibility is to agree with Heaven and be obedient to Heaven's instructions.

If we are in agreement with the ordered steps of the Lord, we can conquer whatever is placed before us.

In the Old Testament, when kings conquered an area, they set about governing it. We should strive to present excellence in our business. As we do so, we conquer the mediocrity that may be present in the marketplace. When we establish a Kingdom business in an area, we are conquering that area for the King. The conquered area has come under the governance of the king who conquered it. That is what *you* will begin to do as you govern your business.

---

*If we formulate the conquering,
it becomes a governing.*

Formulating means methodically creating or devising a strategy or a proposal to express an idea concisely or systematically. Those are two of the definitions.

If we express the idea of conquering systematically through ordered steps, we will be able to govern.

Can two walk together, unless they are agreed? (Amos 3:3)

We should consult Jesus first before we formulate any point or step anywhere on any territory. It must be done via an active agreement because it is an agreement with Jesus.

Seek His will in all you do, and He will show you which path to take. (Proverbs 3:6) (NLT)

If we acknowledge Jesus concisely and systematically, He will direct our paths.

---

*When He directs our paths,
then we can conquer
and then we can govern.*

Jesus has engineered it to be this way. When something has been engineered, it has been skillfully and deliberately arranged rather than arising naturally or spontaneously. Jesus skillfully and deliberately arranges the agreement. We must have ordered steps that express concisely and systematically how we conquer and govern.

The steps of the righteous are ordered by the Lord. (Psalm 37:23)

Or

The steps of the God-pursuing ones follow firmly in the footsteps of the Lord, and God delights in every step they take to follow Him. (Psalms 37:23) (TPT)

The promise of God to Joshua:

I promise you what I promised Moses: 'Wherever you set foot, you will be on land I have given you....' (Joshua 1:3) (NLT)

> *Jesus wants to walk in every place
> we walk in agreement with us.*

> *As we follow His ordered steps,
> our steps are ordered as well.*

We have been busy trying to conquer things ourselves, but the ease is this: He has ordered the steps, but we have to agree with Him.

> *For we are His workmanship, created in Christ Jesus for good works, which God prepared beforehand that we should walk in them. (Ephesians 2:10)*

The Spirit of Excellence

This is where excellence steps in, and this is where the Bond of Excellence is important. We can attempt to produce excellence on our own, or we can step into the entity that is the Spirit of Excellence because this is about ordered steps!

> *We must step into
> the Spirit of Excellence
> and walk in lock step with Jesus
> to conquer our mountain.*

We are not the initiators of these actions—He is. We simply must agree with His direction and be sensitive to it.

Old Paradigms

This method is a whole lot easier than the old method of taking ground through warfare—the swinging of swords and all those things. In the past, people would decide to take a territory or a mountain without discerning if they were supposed to do so. Sometimes, they weren't prepared to do it, or they weren't strong enough to do it. Sometimes, there weren't enough of them to maintain it even if they were successful.

> *Every commandment which I command you today you must be careful to observe, that you may live and multiply, and go in and possess the land of which the LORD swore to your fathers. (Deuteronomy 8:1)*

Many think they can war against principalities the old paradigm way, and they end with so much backlash that people get hurt and end up not standing where they should be. Some have even left the church and given up on intercession because of their experiences of doing things the more difficult way. Jesus modeled the pattern for us:

> *Now I saw Heaven opened, and behold, a white horse. And He who sat on Him was called*

Faithful and True, and in righteousness ***He judges and makes war.*** *(Revelation 19:11)*

We must do the necessary court work to ensure victory on the battlefield. Many have gone to battle, never having inquired of the Lord for the necessary verdict from the Courts of Heaven.

Jesus understands the process— court work first, then battlefield work.

We have found that if we do the proper court work, then the warfare is no longer necessary.

How beautiful are the feet of them that bring good news. (Isaiah 52:7)

We also have to understand that:

Unless we remove the enemy's legal right to be in a place, no permanent effects of our warfare will be experienced.

When engaged with the enemy in warfare, he may simply back off and let you think you won, and then, when you are preoccupied elsewhere, move back in. He has followed that strategy countless times. It's the spiritual warfare fake-out!

Strategized and Ordered Steps

The Father has already strategized and ordered our steps. We need to agree with Him, rather than saying things like, "I don't want to move over there, I don't want to do this, I don't want to do that." These kinds of statements are rebellion. He is saying, "Be yielded to Me, let me bring you into doing what steps I have ordered because Heaven is waiting."

Look at the people who are now being impacted. He is ordering our steps, and all we must do is agree with it and walk in it. Then, see what He does with the beautiful theme of the good news of the gospel of Jesus Christ and the life-changing messages and revelations that He's given so that we don't have to do things the hard way. When He says, "Move," move! When He says, "Stay," stay!

---

*If He has ordered our steps
and we come into agreement with it,
He is actually taking the steps,
not us!*

That is tremendously freeing. It is not unlike a writer, understanding that the books inside of us are already written in Heaven, and all we have to do is engage with Heaven, get the downloads, and translate those downloads into English (or whatever your language is).

Our steps are ordered.

They are already mapped out for us. We don't have to worry or try to devise a plan. We just need to read the scroll or the blueprint. Heaven has made it so easy.

In my book on *Engaging Heaven for Trade*,[32] there is a chapter on "The Golden Pathway," the map that Heaven has designed for our lives. It is laid out before us, and all we need to do is live from our spirit and walk it out. If we get off track somewhere along the way, Heaven has provided those in our cloud of witnesses to work and trade on our behalf to get us back on track.

One of the purposes of gaining the cooperation of our realms is so we can put things in order, govern our realms, and then begin to conquer as sons.

As you have learned, each of your realms has a voice and that voice desires to be recognized and heard. As we do, we will find our lives in better position than ever and better able than ever to order, govern, and conquer. Be blessed as you move forward.

―――― ∞ ――――

---

[32] *Engaging Heaven for Trade* by Dr. Ron M. Horner. (LifeSpring Publishing, 2022)

Chapter 22
Living Trans-dimensionally

Stephanie described what she was seeing as we again engaged Heaven, "I'm standing in front of what looks like a piece of glass made of a prism. It has multiple fragments of light as if you were to look at a diamond ring. I guess the best description is if I'm looking at a mirror that's been broken and its many different shards of glass—that's what it looks like. That's what I'm standing in front of. As I stare at it, I realize it's a tunnel. If I step over this way and look, I can see through the tunnel."

Her Spirit Realm Angel was nearby, and he asked her, "What do you want to do?"

Stephanie replied, "I want to know. I want to learn. Wow! I didn't even have to take a step. I've gone through this portal/tunnel really quickly. I can see way ahead of me as this portal does seem to have an end to it. I'm at the end. Initially, it looks dark on this other end, but I know that's not reality. I would like to know so I can take a step out of this portal and into this dimension.

Spirit Realm Angel asked, "Where are you?"

Stephanie answered, "I feel like I'm in Egypt. In today's time. Am I in modern-day Egypt? I'm standing in a crowded, busy place where they trade and purchase things. I can smell water."

I inserted, "You have the Nile River close by."

She continued, "I hear their dialect. I smell water. Realm Angel, what is this? What have I done?"

Spirit Realm Angel answered, "You've traveled."

Stephanie remarked, "Wow! This *IS* a lesson. I'm just observing the things around me. I see an American woman helping a child. I'm supposed to go in the spirit and lay my hand on her and speak peace."

She walked next to the woman and said, "I speak peace over you, ma'am, and I request, for the angels, lightning bolts of righteousness for her situation. She's some type of missionary. This is bizarre. It's as if she senses something. She's a Christian."

Spirit Realm Angel replied, "Indeed; there are more for you than against you."

Stephanie added, "I feel like I'm being pulled away from this place. I'm standing again in front of this prism of light, the mirror. Malcolm is here."

Malcolm asked, "Well, how did that feel?"

Stephanie replied, "Exhilarating, Malcolm!"

Malcolm remarked, "Baby steps, kid."

Stephanie commented, "Well, Malcolm, that was bigger than a baby step!"

He laughed at her remark and said, "You are indeed trans-dimensional."

Stephanie interjected, "My first question, Malcolm, was about the why. My second question is jurisdiction."

Malcolm explained, "The Earth and the fullness of it belong to the Lord.[33] You **go where he sends you**."

Stephanie remarked, "Interesting. This is why we have been introduced to our Realm Angels, isn't it? Because our Realm Angels will help us dimensionally."

Malcolm replied in the affirmative.

Einstein appeared and asked. "What is quantum?"

Stephanie remarked, "Hi, Einstein. We indeed just walked quantumly. I have been narrow-minded in my thinking because I thought the dimensional talk was about walking in the dimensions of Heaven, but we can do this on Earth, too."

---

[33] Psalm 24:1

Einstein commented, "You must, as sons. It is part of governing. You cannot do this in and of yourselves."

Stephanie shared, "I understand that the kingdom of darkness knows all about this travel stuff, don't they? We have just been so far behind."

Malcolm reinforced, "You are trans-dimensional. This space you walked through, was that in and of yourself?"

Stephanie answered, "No."

Einstein asked, "Who goes before you?"

Stephanie replied, "The Word. Heaven just taught us that."

Malcolm remarked, "*You only go where He sends you.*"

Stephanie added, "I think my carefulness with this, Malcolm, is just a matter of principle for people to understand that they cannot use this in any form or fashion other than when the Word is going before them and only going where He sends them. But we have to be willing because otherwise, it's no different than the kingdom of darkness in how they do this."

Einstein opened his hand and held out two marbles.

She asked, "What are these for?"

Einstein replied, "Look deeper."

Stephanie remarked, "It's a realm inside of these. Am I supposed to take these, or am I just looking at them?"

Einstein asked, "Did I create these?"

Stephanie answered, "I don't know."

He put them in his pocket and reminded her of when we saw several doors a while back. She commented, "I stepped into a place, and there were doors all around me. I opened one of them and I went into my past, to a time when a boy had been so ugly to me.[34] I ended up praying for and forgiving him. This is that place. All these doors are places that we are called to go to. Is this correct, Malcolm and Einstein?

Malcolm asked, "Did you go and relegate the past?"

Stephanie asked, "What is relegate?"

I replied, "To send into exile. Banish, put out of mind to an appropriate place or situation based on classification or appraisal to transfer.

She continued, "I relegated the old; I went back to that place, saw something, and changed it, didn't I? Did I relegate the past?"

"Yes," Malcolm responded.

---

[34] More about this in the next chapter.

"What did I do today?" She asked. "I observed, released, and only went where I was called for the Kingdom's sake."

Malcolm remarked,

---
*This is intercession
on a different level.*

Stephanie commented, "When I saw this woman, I imparted something to her that she needed. I didn't even know her."

Malcolm explained, "This is governing. Are you willing?"

Stephanie replied, "Yes."

Malcolm asked, "How many say, 'I want you Lord, I want to go where you want me to go.' This is part of the plan. Are you willing?"

Stephanie reaffirmed, "Yes."

Malcolm explained, "The people perish for their lack of knowledge."[35]

Stephanie continued, "I understand that it's not just about us perishing as if something happened. By

---

[35] Hosea 4:6

imparting something to this lady, we are helping others not to perish because we have gained knowledge."

Malcolm remarked, "It gives a whole new spin on praying for somebody else, doesn't it?"

Stephanie replied, "Yes. I didn't even know her."

Malcolm added, "Baby steps."

Stephanie continued, "Thank you, Malcolm. Show me more! Thank you, Einstein and my Realm Angel. Angel, how do we commission you?"

We were told that we are to commission them dimensionally, as originally taught, and request that they show us spiritually where we can live, move, and have our being. Stephanie then gave her angel a commissioning:

I commission you, angel, to the trans-dimensional work of my spirit. Go where the Father sends me to do this, for the Word to go before me as it opens portals.

———·———

Chapter 23
Being Trans-dimensional

As we began our engagement with Heaven, Stephanie remarked, "We would like to know more about trans-relocation." The events of the previous chapter regarding being trans-dimensional had occurred very recently.

Stephanie promptly found herself in what appeared to be Fort Knox, where a large repository of gold is kept for the United States government.

Malcolm remarked, "The question is, 'Could you have gotten here any other way?'"

She replied, "No, I could not have gotten here any other way."

Malcolm asked, "What did you do to arrive here?"

She answered, "I just submitted. That was one of the things to do, right? I just submitted, right? I just submitted. I didn't even have to see a portal; I was just here; I'm here—I'm still here. How was I able to do that?

"All of a sudden, I went far out of this room in Fort Knox, and I could see 'me' standing over there. Of course, I'm not sure which me is seeing that me over there?"

She continued, "Do you remember the teaching we had about 'what you can see, you can govern?'[36] The pinpoint precision of looking forward and then down at where your feet are—you've got to govern that territory. When I went outside of Fort Knox, I could see into it, and I knew that what I could see, I could govern."

What I can see, I can govern.

Malcolm remarked, "You live, and you move, and you have your being in Him." The caution is to go only when He sends you where He sends you.

Stephanie added, "It's like the day David went to a couple's house in the spirit. He was sitting in the Sunday service and suddenly was in their home."

I commented, "Well, Isaiah 60:8 says, "Who are these who fly like a cloud and like doves to the roost" or Isaiah 40:31, "And the Lord shall renew their strength,

---

[36] See the blog "Governing 101" at RonHorner.com.

they shall mount up with wings like eagles, they shall run and not be weary and walk and not faint.'

"Ian Clayton mentioned in a video clip on trans-relocation that Ezekiel also experienced it. He traveled about 1500 miles. Phillip traveled from where he was in Gaza to Azotus, which is about 27 miles."

Trans-relocation is when your body, soul, and spirit are moved to another place, another time, or the same time.

All our realms go, not just our spirit man. All of us find ourselves somewhere. When Phillip was found in Azotus, he was probably thinking, 'How did I get here?'

Stephanie remarked, "I'm just realizing that I have had this experience before. Okay—when my daughter, Angelina, was a little younger than four, we went to a church meeting. My husband was passed out drunk in the house. I packed her up and I went to this little church meeting on a Wednesday night and the preacher talked about covenant relationship. It was the first time I ever understood covenant. He was saying that we break covenant as Westerners, but God never breaks covenant. You know, these are the things he talked about, like relationships that you would be in and sexual immorality and those kinds of things—it's a type of breaking covenant.

"Well, I get in the car, and I have an actual experience where I'm suspended in air in a room. It's like I'm literally suspended, and I'm wrapped in chains. Small chains, big chains, long chain, small chains—and they were for every person that I had a wrong relationship with or created a soul tie with. I began to repent, speak their name, and the chain would fall off. At the end, I was free. Now, I had a 30-minute drive because I went to a church in Memphis and I lived in Olive Branch, Mississippi.

"When I pulled out of the driveway of the church was when I began this suspension in air. After I had that experience, when I came out of it, I was in my garage. I was there in less than the 30-minute period of time it would have taken me to get home. It wasn't that long. Wow! That was my whole body being trans-relocated and so was my daughter—and my car!"

I remarked, "If you go back and look at your timeline, you will see that you jumped ahead of time. If you think back, is the drive home missing from your mind?"

Stephanie replied, "It is, indeed."

I mentioned an occasion when we pastored a church in Wilson, North Carolina. We had some friends coming from Raleigh to see us in Wilson and the wife was driving their car. On the way, the husband had fallen asleep, and the wife got mixed up, made a couple of wrong turns and ended up going back toward Raleigh.

I called and woke him up to find out when they expected to arrive. He described where they were when he had her make a turn off the highway. They were 25 minutes from where we lived but instead of being 25 minutes away, they were immediately in our driveway. As I recall, I was on the phone with them, talking about where they were, and I knew where they were and where we were—about 25 minutes apart, and just a moment later they were in our driveway.

Albert Einstein appeared at this point in our engagement, and we asked what else we were to learn.

Stephanie asked him, recalling when she was in Fort Knox and saw herself looking at herself, "What am I to see about where I'm standing?"

Describing what she saw, she said, "In my perspective, I see a dimension difference. The scenery changed again, as you can imagine. Now, there's a third part of me looking at the second part of me that's looking at the first part of me. But what I'm seeing from the second and the first part of me is that the second part of me is in a dimension that is higher than the Fort Knox first part of me, and that dimension is lower. I'm seeing myself from this dimension looking at that dimension."

Einstein remarked, "You are indeed trans-dimensional."

He continued, "How many heavens are there?"

"Twelve that I know of," she replied.

Einstein asked, "Can you be in all twelve simultaneously?"

"I believe so—now," she answered.

"Would you like to be?" He questioned.

She excitedly replied, "Yes, please!"

Describing what immediately transpired, she said, "I'm standing at a door. I see twelve of me."

"There's something to be said about submissiveness. What do you do at a door?" He asked.

"You open it," she answered. "I see myself opening a door from the bottom of the twelve heavens. It started at the bottom and happened fast. The next one opened the next one, and it opened the next one, which opened the next one, continuing until all the doors were open."

Instead of them all doing it at the same exact time, a slight delay (but only milliseconds) occurred so she could grasp what was happening.

Einstein asked, "Do you believe you could walk in all twelve dimensions simultaneously?"

Stephanie replied, "Well, you're asking me that a second time. Yes, I do."

"What frame of reference could you have to take in all twelve experiences simultaneously?" He inquired.

"I don't pretend to know," she answered. "Is it in the delay of each millisecond? Is that where I could quickly retain what happened in door number one and then retain what happened in door number two? Is that what we're talking about here?"

He reiterated, "The question is: what frame of reference?"

She explained, "I feel like this is a simple answer I'm missing because I'm making it a bigger frame of reference than it needs to be. Wisdom, I invoke you. Understanding and knowledge, I need you.

"Frame of reference—I get it; each of these are a picture of a frame of reference. You know how when you take photographs and it clicks really fast and takes them really fast? Each picture is a specific frame capturing the next detail of what's going on.

"Can you help us, Einstein, with the frame of reference?"

Einstein asked, "What do you see?"

She replied, "I see twelve different snapshots of me opening a door, but just slightly different, timewise—if we are thinking about time."

He queried, "Is it? Or is it just how your frame of reference captured that image?"

Stephanie answered, "Okay; these are not things of the mind, but of the spirit—I get it."

She added, "The twelve heavens are *in* Him. I made the twelve heavens big and scary in my mind, like they're unattainable, but we've only scratched the surface! It's so much and it's massive. It is more than we can think or imagine, but it's IN Him. Since we live and move and have our being in Him, we can be in each of those places, move from each of those places, and have our being in each of those places simultaneously!"

I interjected, "That's why we're learning to coordinate our realms so that the 3-D thinking doesn't overwhelm the soul thinking."

Stephanie added, "I was thinking of it initially like, 'Oh, that's my spirit in Fort Knox, and that is my soul standing outside of it looking in.' But no, like you said, 'Think quantum.'"

You can go into the most dangerous and secure places if called.

Ezekiel's Travels

We often miss that Ezekiel the prophet experienced translocation and/or trans-relocation many times, more than any other recorded person in the Bible:

- Ezekiel 3:12—when he heard a loud voice saying, "Blessed is the Glory of the LORD from His place."
- Two verses later, the Spirit of the Lord lifted him up and took him away.
- In chapter 8, verse 3, the Spirit of the Lord lifted him up and suspended him in midair while he was shown some things, then took him to the north gate of the inner court.
- In Ezekiel 11:1, the Spirit of the Lord lifted him up and brought him to the East Gate of the LORD's house.
- In Ezekiel 43:5, he was again lifted and brought to the East Gate, where he was shown the real leaders of Jerusalem.

Isaiah spoke of this in Isaiah 60:8:

Who are these who fly like a cloud, And like doves to their roosts?

And in Isaiah 40:31:

But those who wait on the LORD Shall renew their strength; they shall mount up with wings like eagles, they shall run and not be weary, they shall walk and not faint.

Elijah ran supernaturally fast, as is recorded in 1 Kings 18:46.

The caution is to be led by your spirit and not your soul; however, Heaven did not make it hard—we do.

We are so accustomed to our 3-dimensional thinking and 3-D realm that our soul struggles to let us out of that box. However, by learning to live from our spirit with our spirit in the forwardmost position, we can break free of the constraints of 3-D thinking. We can seek those things that are above, as Paul taught us in Colossians 3:2:

> *Becoming affectionately acquainted with throne room thoughts will keep you from being distracted again by the earthly, soul-ruled realm. (THE MIRROR)*

These experiences are not for personal Brownie points; they are not to boost your ego, and they are not to build your personal kingdom in any way.

The simplicity of Spirit travel is amazing. You only need to submit to the will of the Father. We are trans-dimensional, and where the Holy Spirit takes us is not in and of ourselves; it is the Father's doing. By going where He sends us, we protect ourselves from going where our souls may want to go. Translocation is when your spirit is taken to another locale.

We are trans-dimensional, but we cannot do this spirit travel in and of ourselves. We only go where the Father sends us. Otherwise, our behavior is the same as that of those who serve Satan. Also, we are not speaking of astral projection, which is the projection of one's soul into another place, realm, or dimension.

As discussed in the previous chapter, Stephanie was talking with Einstein and she was reminded of another engagement with Heaven when she saw many doors before her. She stepped through one and was taken back to a time as a child when a boy at school was bullying her. She saw Jesus inserted into the situation, and the boy's behavior changed entirely. In that encounter, Stephanie forgave the boy for his behavior, and she was shown what was driving him to behave as he did. His home life was broken, and when she saw that, she could forgive him.

The past can be changed by encounters where we step back in time and affect change as led by the Holy Spirit.

Trans-dimensional travel is not just about the present. It can affect the past, present, and future. In this way, we can relegate the past. We can banish it and its impact upon us, and we can be healed and restored.

Stephanie realized that in today's encounter, she observed the situation she found herself in, released only what she was instructed to release, and went only where she was called to go for the sake of the Kingdom. It was *intercession on a different level.*

When Stephanie saw the woman in the marketplace, she imparted something to her that she needed, even though she did not know the woman. It was a type of governing.

Are we willing to govern in that manner?

How many will say, "I want you, Lord. I want to go where you want me to go," and are willing to be led entirely by Him?

On this subject, people perish due to a lack of knowledge, but knowledge is forthcoming. In Stephanie's encounter, she imparted something to this lady and subsequently helped others not to perish because she had gained knowledge.

This gives a whole new spin on praying for someone else, doesn't it?

We can commission our Realm Angel, particularly our Spirit Realm Angel, to help us dimensionally and show us spiritually where we can live, move, and have our being.[37]

I commission you, angel, to the trans-dimensional work of my spirit to go where the Father sends me to do this and for the Word to go before me as it opens portals.

Our Realm Angel for our spirit would be the angel to assist us in this extended form of intercession. As I mentioned earlier in this chapter, spirit travel was recorded in Acts 8 when Philip, upon instruction from

---

[37] Acts 17:28

Heaven, met the Ethiopian eunuch. Upon ministering to and baptizing him, he was caught away—spirit, soul, AND body—and found about thirty miles away in Azotus.

How do we facilitate spirit traveling?

- First, realize many of you are already traveling in the spirit when you engage with Heaven.
- Remember, You only go where He wants you to go.
- Do not be overwhelmed when it happens.
- Do not let your soul take over. You are there in the spirit; we go when he says go—we cannot manipulate. That is the biggest thing.
- We cannot manipulate situations by going just because we want to go.

Stephanie said, "I have a question for Heaven because I want to go to North Carolina."

Heaven replied that she was already in North Carolina (where I live), and I was in Germantown (where she lived) simultaneously.

The question to answer is: "Are you willing?"

It is about submission and being willing, but we cannot be willy-nilly either.

- Yieldedness to the will of the Father to be available to be sent.

- Yieldedness to be available to go as He directs.
- Willingness to cooperate and not manipulate the "where."
- Willingness to follow Father's instructions.
- Willingness to keep it private if directed.

———·———

Chapter 24
Mastering the Mind

Recently, Stephanie and I were made aware of a different class of angels known as Realm Angels. These angels are assigned to each individual, and there are Realm Angels for one's soul, one's spirit, and one's body. They bring alignment and work dimensionally. One of their functions is to clean up the debris left in our lives from wrong relationships—and we have *all* had wrong relationships.

Their appearance resembles Tinkerbell from the animated Disney® movies; however, they are not small like Tinkerbell but human-sized. Their wings may be effervescent in color.

They can also teach us about their roles, increasing our understanding. As we engaged Heaven, one of Stephanie's Realm Angels began teaching us. We found ourselves in the Library of Revelation and were instructed to be seated.

The Soul Realm Angel brought a book titled *Before the Foundations of the Earth* to the table. Stephanie turned the page and was transported to when the Father had a conversation with each of her realms before the Earth's foundations. As the conversation ended, each realm stepped into the other of her realms, becoming one. The Father began speaking to the Soul Realm Angels as well. It was as if she was watching a bubble merge with another bubble as you would do with a child's liquid bubble toy. Each angel stepped into each bubble, and now, they were one. The Father took the one bubble, leaned over, and kissed it.

Suddenly, she was back in the room. When Stephanie asked for an explanation of where she was now, the Soul Realm Angel replied, "This is where the Father originally constructed you." Stephanie knew these Soul Realm Angels had been with her since the beginning.

She began hearing the word 'escapism.' "What is that?" She asked.

I replied, "Escapism is doing things to distract yourself from what's happening around you. People do that with TV and movies."

The Soul Realm Angel instructed her to read the text on the page. She read, "Escapism is powerless, mind-numbing and futile. The instruction of the Lord to these angels is **to bring us out of escapism.**"

The Soul Realm Angel asked, "Would you say the mind can be fragmented?"

"Yes," Stephanie replied.

The Soul Realm Angel continued, "Is gathering the bits and pieces of the fragmentations part of dimensional work, going into different dimensions?"

She replied, "Yes, we're aware of that, but we have been thinking that only their souls have been fragmented."

The Soul Realm Angel answered, "That is true, but these thoughts have been held captive. A person is unable to get past those thoughts. Our dimensional work brings back these thoughts of escapism."

The Soul Realm Angel instructed her, "Read the text."

"We know that spirit and soul can be fragmented and taken into different dimensions and realms, but what is the purpose of this understanding?" Stephanie responded.

The Soul Realm Angel replied, "It is our job to help minister to the fragments and bring them back. We can help **master the mind**."

"How so?" Stephanie asked.

The Soul Realm Angel asked, "Can all things be explained?"

"In the natural, I would say no," she responded.

The Soul Realm Angel inquired, "Can all things be explained?"

She replied, "Can we explain all of the fragmentation?"

The Soul Realm Angel further queried, "Where is truth?"

Stephanie said, "Truth is here in Heaven. Truth is Jesus and His Word."

The Soul Realm Angel explained, "We are to bring back the truth. Can you 'master the mind' if you have the truth?"

Stephanie questioned, "Isn't the mind the soul?"

The Soul Realm Angel countered, "Is it? Our job is to help master the mind. What are you instructed to take captive?"

"Our thoughts," she replied.

The Apostle Paul said, 2 Corinthians 10:3-6:

> *³ For though we walk in the flesh, we do not war according to the flesh. ⁴ For the weapons of our warfare are not carnal but mighty in God for pulling down strongholds, ⁵ casting down arguments and every high thing that exalts itself against the knowledge of God, bringing every thought into captivity to the obedience of Christ,*

⁶ and being ready to punish all disobedience when your obedience is fulfilled.

The Soul Realm Angel asked, "Would you say you've been good at that?"

Stephanie responded, "I plead the fifth[38]. I have not been exceptionally good at that, no."

The angel asked, "What if you had help?"

"Well, I have been taught that the Holy Spirit helps us in that," Stephanie remarked.

The Soul Realm Angel answered, "We acknowledge that He is, but are there not more for you than against you?"

She inquired, "How do you help us master the mind?"

The Soul Realm Angel asked, "Who is over the soul?"

"Jesus," she answered.

Realm Angel queried, "Is His Word not a calming effect on the mind?

"It is," she replied.

The Soul Realm Angel asked, "If 'Thy word is a lamp into thy feet and a light into that path,' why have you

---

[38] Pleading the 5th is an American expression referring to the 5th Amendment of the United States Constitution about not having to incriminate yourself.

not mastered the mind? If you have not mastered the mind, would you say all are fragmented to Escapism?"

Stephanie asked, "Are you saying *all*?"

The Soul Realm Angel instructed, "Turn the page."

As she did, the Soul Realm Angel explained, "Our instruction is to bring the complete work of Jesus Christ to the mind, the heart, and the unit that is the body. We do this dimensionally."

She asked, "How do we instruct you?"

The Soul Realm Angel replied, "As you have been, by directing us to work dimensionally. **Mastering the mind is not intellect; it is submission**. Who do you think can take things captive and tear down strongholds?"

She remarked, "You help us with that, right?"

"Per your instruction, we are a help in time of need," was the response.

Stephanie added, "I have a question about mastering the mind since we are to live by the spirit."

The Soul Realm Angel asked, "Is your mind not in full play?"

"Yes, it is."

"Then master the mind. It is not in and of yourselves; it is the work of the Lord," the Soul Realm Angel responded.

> *Soul Realm Angels will help
> bring down strongholds
> and are a very present help
> in time of need.*

Stephanie exclaimed, "I have a lot of questions! I just got a picture of how we have been numbing ourselves and our children at very early ages and teaching escapism instead of intimacy—by sitting them in front of the TV, handing them a tablet, and so on."

I asked the Soul Realm Angel, "What is the process?"

The Soul Realm Angel remarked, "I thought you would never ask."

Stephanie commented, "I realize I have a huge religious spirit mindset around this—it's trying to cause and inflict fear. I lay that down; I'm willing to hear the truth."

The Soul Realm Angel asked, "What is adjudication?"

"It is doing the necessary court work," I replied.

Turning to Stephanie, the Soul Realm Angel asked, "What was on your mind upon waking up today?"

She replied, "The word I heard this morning was 'principled.' The definition of principled is 'acting in accordance with morality and showing recognition of right and wrong based on a given set of rules.'

"Angel, in our processes of court work, is this where we present our mind to the Lord? What is this process? My mind keeps going back to the scripture, where we are to take our thoughts captive to the obedience of Christ. What is the best way to do that?

The Soul Realm Angel instructed, "Commission us."

Stephanie described what she was seeing: "I see them helping us take captive our thoughts and things that are speaking into our lives, spirit, soul. They are helping to take these things captive. They are capturing—literally capturing things. Is that what we're to do?"

The Soul Realm Angel replied, **"We are your very help in times of trouble."**

Stephanie prayed,

I ask the Father to forgive me for escapism. I have done it my entire life. I've taught my children to do it, and, in the worldly sense, I have helped put them in captivity and put myself in captivity through escapism. I would like to be free from that, please. I repent, Father, and I ask for the blood of Jesus and the amendment of 'As If It Never Were' and that you forgive me.

I request the angels to help master my mind around this and take captive these thoughts that come, those that are not of the Lord. I instruct you to do this in the mighty name of Jesus.

Jesus, thank you. Father, thank you for putting these angels with me before the foundations of the world. I'm grateful that there's more for us than against us. This is truly dimensional.

Angel, I commission you to do your work dimensionally around this, taking captive all of these thoughts and shutting the door to escapism that I've opened in every dimension.

The Soul Realm Angel remarked, "How many have truly beat themselves up because they cannot control their thoughts?"

She answered, "Well, that's true, but we have been doing much court work for this. Isn't that closing the door to generational sins?"

I asked, "How can we do it more effectively?"

"Close the door on escapism," the Soul Realm Angel replied.

Stephanie governed,

In Jesus' name, I close every portal and every door that the enemy has used against my life and my dimensions. I close the door of escapism.

The Soul Realm Angel spoke, "Would you say that, for many, food is a form of escapism? Music is escapism. TV is escapism. Reading books full of pornography and the way of the world is escapism."

"It is, it is. It is," Stephanie responded.

The Soul Realm Angel reiterated, "Close the door to escapism."

Stephanie began a commission to the Soul Realm Angel:

I commission you to close the door in all the dimensions, as I have adjudicated to the Lord these sins that have been in my life. I repent on behalf of my generations. I bring the generations in. We have all used escapism, which has been a lie from the enemy. Forgive us, Lord. I know that we're not going to get super sanctimonious in this.

She clarified, "It's okay to watch TV. It's okay to chill but being consumed by it is what the Soul Realm Angel talks about."

The Soul Realm Angel replied, "There will be more. These are *baby steps.*"

"Well, we look forward to more training," Stephanie remarked.

The angel then closed the book, put it back on the shelf, and came over and went inside her, saying, "Master the mind. It is where you can truly have your thoughts taken captive quickly, efficiently, and effectively, and not live in that bondage, but remember you can't do it by yourself."

———— ∞ ————

Chapter 25

Wielding the Sword of Resolve

Have you ever given thought to how much resolve Noah must have possessed to spend 120 years building an ark to load with a sampling of all the animals in preparation for a flood that had never been experienced before? It must have taken great strength of character. It also took strength to realize that all you had ever known, nearly everyone you had ever known, was going to exist only as a memory in the future.

After spending over a year on the ark, his first act was to build an altar and make a sacrifice to the Lord. Do you think he was wearied at that time, or was he resolved?

Resolve is the firm determination to do something. It is firmly deciding on a course of action. The long ordeal was now over. The question is—how do you think he felt about being right?

I imagine he had a *good resolve,* but how is resolve built?

It is built by seeing the faithfulness of God.

Has resolve been built in you?

We would like to think so because we probably have resolve on many levels, but we also think about other challenges.

Do you think Noah knew there would be challenges? Of course. We need to treat resolve as a wielding sword. It's a placement in our spirit versus our soul or body realm.

If you wield resolve as a sword, it cuts away the doubt that infringes.[39]

Doubt *infringes* on people. We must learn to wield the sword of resolve and do it properly; then, we will experience victory.

Resolve is an important factor.

---

[39] Infringe: Actively break the terms of (a law, agreement. Violate, breach, transgress, break) (Oxford Dictionary)

In mathematics, a factor is any of the numbers or symbols that, when multiplied together, form a product. In this case, it forms the product of the sword.

It's also a number or symbol that divides another number or symbol. The situations we face are *symbols*. The sword can divide the symbol.

I request the factor of resolve to be wielded as a sword from my spirit in Jesus' name.

I request resolve for my spirit to wield it like a sword, cutting away all doubt that infringes.

I am in unity and harmony, so I know that my soul and body are in unison with this.

I charge the spirit angels of my realms to help me wield the sword of resolve.

I ask, Father (since you are Lord over my Spirit), that You would help me wield the factor of resolve within my spirit that will then teach my soul and then my body. My soul and body are one with my spirit.

As the prayer above was prayed, a huge angel showed up and presented a glorious sword shining brightly. We each took the sword and put it on our spirit.

———— ∞ ————

Chapter 26

Maximizing

"As If It Never Were"

Those of you who have been tracking with LifeSpring have heard us refer to the Merry Maids of Heaven—angels who clean up spiritual debris in people and places. They can handle all types of spiritual debris and obstructions.

Philippians 4:13 declares "I can do ALL things through Christ who strengthens me."

The Passion Translation reads, "I find that the strength of Christ's explosive power infuses me to conquer every difficulty."

The question is: "What are 'ALL things?'"

This is about sonship. The work that we're doing allows for all spiritual debris, all things that need to be cleaned up, to be cleaned up as we delegate through our sonship that Jesus died for.

During one of our engagements in Heaven with Malcolm, he asked us, "What is the significant use of these Merry Maids?"

We know that they clean up spiritual debris, but what else? We were about to learn.

We first learned about the amendment of "As If It Never Were" a few months before when we were dealing with a former employee and the debris the person had left behind in the ministry. Alicia, our heavenly Personnel Director, asked us if, concerning that situation, we wanted Heaven to make it "as if it never were." We said yes, and then she gave the folder to an angel who disappeared. In the natural arena, the situation calmed down.

A few months later, we were taught about some more of the implications of this powerful amendment. Heaven had told us that this amendment was far more powerful than we recognized.

Heaven asked, "What is the amendment of 'As If It Never Were?' Would you not consider that there's an element of sweeping to be done?

"In the amendment of 'As If It Never Were,' what is the element?"

Heaven asked, "What is a filament?"

Stephanie replied, "One type of filament is the thin wire inside of a light bulb."

Heaven asked, "What is a conduit?"

Stephanie continued, "A conduit is a passageway for something else."

If all things work together through Christ that strengthens us, how would the element (the filament), and the conduit work together?"

It provides illumination. When you have an element, a filament, and a conduit, it brings light in the natural, correct? The conduit allows the current to flow to the filament, which then expresses to the light bulb element.

Heaven asked another question, "Are you the light of the world?"

With that question, Stephanie realized that *people* are the element in this discussion. Then the question became, *what is the filament?*

The answers were given through the example of a chess game.

The pieces are the element, the conduit is the movement of pieces on the board, and the filament is one's willingness to play the game. By our very will, we can choose or not choose to be the reason for the agreement to be *on board* with the Father who is teaching us now by using a chess board.

Our very act of agreement is the filament with which all of Heaven can use to move the element.

What do the Merry Maid angels have to do with any of this?

It *is* by our agreement and choosing to utilize them to clean up the mess. We use these terms for the sake of understanding; however, it is an act of agreement, and by your own will to clean up the generations, to undo a sin the minute you do it—agree!

I agree to be the element using my will, in agreement with Heaven, for Heaven to be the conduit into my life. I choose to co-labor with the Merry Maid angels as they clean up the debris in my life.

Let's talk about Jonah. Was it his very act of will to be put in the belly of a whale?

No. So then, where did his will come in?

He exercised his will when he chose to disobey, and then the Father provided a way for him to change his mind and do the Father's will. The conduit (of the belly of the whale) helped him change his mind.

In this scenario, **Jonah is the element**. He went and did the work of the Lord. But the question is: Did he fulfill his destiny?

Stephanie noted Jonah was mad afterward, especially after God didn't destroy Nineveh.

Malcolm asked, "Wouldn't you say that would require some cleanup work?"

"Yes!" Stephanie replied.

Dr. Rodich's Input

It all started about a month ago as I sat in my chair. I kept hearing, "The soul is more than you think." I thought, "Well, okay." I went on my merry way, sat back, studied for the evening, fell asleep, and kept hearing, "This soul is more than you think." I have been on this journey, and I've had a lot of help from my wife, Stephanie, my friend Brian, and others.

We are finding out how God put His hand into the elements of the Earth. The order in which we are made is very interesting. The soul was made before the body, which appeared as that silver-looking liquid we spoke of previously. The soul then attracted the elements of the Earth that became man's flesh and bone.

I said, "Okay, that's fine, but the soul isn't lit up yet." That happened when it says that God breathed. (Just an amusing side point: God doesn't need to breathe.) When He expresses whatever would be considered His breath, it has all kinds of design, blueprints, glory, and fire. He breathes into Adam and gives him the operating system. Basically, the body and soul were in place, and God breathed into Adam. The man lights up, and the operating system goes live. It's like the first time you plug your computer in, and you turn it on for the first time, and everything powers up, and it's like, "Okay, we are ready to go."

What we are looking at here is trying to define a lot of the damage that has taken place in the soul, which created the mess many of us find ourselves in. If I used the term 'fracturing,' everyone would go, "Oh yeah, that's somebody that's got DID[40] or they've been in Satanic Ritual Abuse." But what happens if we accept anything that isn't the design of our personal spirit? We're fractured.

We discovered that even if you wipe the slate clean, which I did (I walked around like a zombie for two days because I couldn't figure out who I was), that...

Our soul and our body are to be the demonstrated ambassadors for God's Kingdom.

Suddenly, we were told about bringing our spirit forward—that is who we really are. Then we find out that our soul and our body serve another purpose, and that's to be the demonstrated ambassadors for God's Kingdom, His emotional or Quantum Emotional Realm, and everything He is. We're supposed to be ambassadors, but we cannot be effective without all these other filters and static interference.

A few days ago, I said, "Lord, there's still some stuff going on, but I can't pin it down. How does this relate to

---

[40] Dissociative Identity Disorder

the things we have been learning?" Suddenly, He showed me—in this case, He was speaking to me about my body, but the same thing rings true for the soul; you can get rid of the trauma, you can get rid of the energy factors, you can say all the denouncement prayers, and they work. It all works.

Cellular Memory & More

Organs can retain memory. Have any of you heard the story of a person who had a heart transplant that came from somebody who was murdered? The memory of that murder and what the perpetrators looked like was imprinted on the heart so that when the person who received the transplant testified in court, the judge accepted their testimony, and the criminals were convicted of murder.

If the heart can retain memory, we know the digestive system can, and several other organs likely can. You may say, "Well, I've been prayed for a million times."

What if we have been healed, but the one thing left is the memory? The same goes for the soul. You do all this work—God's there, the angels are there, everything's there—but you've got to clean up the memories.

That's the newest and latest revelation—I'm sure there will be other things the Lord will show us. What if the healing was there, but because there were other factors we didn't know of at that moment, the healing didn't manifest? Getting the cleanup angels to help you with the memories—could be that breakthrough that you've been waiting through for a long time?

∞

One morning, in my (Ron speaking) journaling time, Heaven shared this with me:

> *You have learned a little about the amendment of 'As If It Never Were,' but so much more is to be learned. Heaven alluded to that months ago, but you were not ready to receive it. I have uncovered some things for Dr. Rodich because he was seeking to understand, and that has led you to a new place in your understanding of how this can be applied to cellular memory and memories of the soul and spirit.*
>
> *Each has memories that can either enhance or hinder life. When your soul, for example, holds memories of disappointment due to perceived unanswered prayers, those memories will try to dictate how faith is applied in the future. They will try to dictate whether one will come into agreement with Heaven or not.*
>
> *For instance, as in past cases you have worked with, the body realm is disappointed because it thinks God did not keep His promise. But Numbers 23:19 plainly describes the integrity of*

the Father. It is reiterated in Matthew 7 when Jesus said, 'If you ask, you receive.' Neither the Father nor Jesus have gone back on their promise. The prayers have been answered, but the receipt of the answer has been hindered. The soul has limited the receipt of the provision, the healing, and the promise based on memories from the past.

Hebrews 6:17-19:

> [17] Thus God, determining to show more abundantly to the heirs of promise the immutability of His counsel, confirmed it by an oath,
>
> [18] that by two immutable things, in which **it is impossible for God to lie**, we might have strong consolation, who have fled for refuge to lay hold of the hope set before us.
>
> [19] This **hope** we have as **an anchor of the soul**, both sure and steadfast, and which enters the Presence behind the veil,

It has clung to those memories, making them trophies of failure and excuses for why the Father did not come through when He did. His response came from Heaven into your realm, but you have not understood the power of realm memories to hinder things flowing into your life.

When Paul wrote, 'You have the mind of Christ,' he inferred that one aspect of Christ's mind is *that realm-related memories are not limiters to the supply of Heaven.*

He never prayed a prayer that was not answered. Neither have you. The teaching that God answers every prayer—sometimes yes and sometimes no—is built on the disappointment in the soul or body (usually the soul) to what it perceives as unanswered prayers. No, I promised if you asked, you would receive it. You have built theologies and belief systems that are outside the Word based on your experiences or perceived experiences you have had.

Remember the story of the crippled man at the Pool of Bethesda? His memories of past failures were affecting his motivation to keep trying.

John 5:1-9

> *¹ Then Jesus returned to Jerusalem to observe one of the Jewish holy days.*
>
> *² Inside the city near the Sheep Gate there is a pool called in Aramaic,* **The House of Loving Kindness.** *And this pool is surrounded by five covered porches.*
>
> *³ Hundreds of* **sick people were lying there** *on the porches—the paralyzed, the blind, and the crippled, all of them* **waiting for their healing.**
>
> *⁴ For an angel of God would periodically descend into the pool to stir the waters, and the first one who stepped into the pool*

after the waters swirled would instantly be healed.

⁵ Now there was a man who had been disabled for thirty-eight years lying among the multitude of the sick.

⁶ When Jesus saw him lying there, He knew that the man had been crippled for a long time. So, Jesus said to him, "Do you truly long to be healed?"

⁷ The sick man answered Him, "Sir, there's no way I can get healed, for I have no one who will lower me into the water when the angel comes. As soon as I try to crawl to the edge of the pool, someone else jumps in ahead of me."

⁸ Then Jesus said to him, "Stand up! Pick up your sleeping mat, and you will walk!"

*⁹ Immediately **he stood up—he was healed!** So he rolled up his mat and walked again!*

His body realm was so disappointed that he had not been able to get into the water in time that he had all but given up.

Hope deferred makes a heart sick. (Proverbs 13:12)

Dr. Rodich is compiling more information on this so we aren't going to unpack it yet, but soon.

Back to the Merry Maids.

How do we use this practically?

- Repent where we have redefined our belief system to explain our experiences.
- Repent where we have judged the Father in His perceived handling of our situations.
- Repent where we have become the Father's judge, AND
- Repent where we have become other's judges when they would not change their faith expression to go along with us.

When you have done a lot of the work generationally, the spiritual debris that's left behind can use some cleanup, and the amendment of "As If It Never Were" is how you do that. You can instruct the angels, these Merry Maids of Heaven, to clean up the spiritual debris as the amendment of "As If It Never Were" is being implemented.

This is necessary because, even though you've done the generational work, you still have residue from the decisions and will of the men involved. This provides a way to fully clarify things. It's all about unveiling and unpacking.

Let's commission the angels to this:

I call the Merry Maids of Heaven regarding all the places on record where I have done repentance, lineage, and generational work. I request the amendment of 'As If It

Never Were.' I request that they clean up the spiritual debris, burn it, and give it to Jesus.

---∞---

Chapter 27
Script for Aligning Your Realms

We are sharing the following script to activate your realms to cooperate with one another and to activate the angels of our realms and our personal angels to work together in unity and harmony. Please feel free to make this part of your daily prayer routine as you grow in your sonship. Scripts often help us as we learn a concept and implement it into our lives. Allow Heaven to give input to you so that it becomes fine-tuned to your life. Don't allow it to become a rote recitation that has no life within it. Remember to call your angels near as you follow this script so they can assist in its implementation.

The segment Declaration for the Soul helps you begin the process of aligning your realms. Our soul has a neutralizing effect on our spirit and needs to be positioned rightly. This segment seeks to assist with that.

Declaration for the Soul

I submit my free will to the will of the Father.

Using my free will, I speak perfect cohesiveness to my soul to serve as the axis point to protect my DNA.

Using my free will, spirit, I charge you to take the things that you receive from God and Heaven and place them into my heart. I expand my heart to scan the things coming from my spirit, God, and Heaven, and I commission my Heart to look at the options and choices and run them through the processes of Heaven. Now, transfer these things the way Heaven intended into my soul.

Soul, you are born from above and are grounded in a new heavenly system and design. Now, release the DNA design of Jesus the Messiah into my DNA, pass His information to my RNA, and regulate cellular function at the highest possible level.

I acknowledge that Jesus the Messiah is seated in my soul in full government and authority. His Presence moves me from the corruptible to the incorruptible.

Soul, because Jesus Himself has become the source of your design, I am now free to release His light, sound, glory, fire, and living water to my body, to others, and into creation—as we only do what we see Father doing.

Soul, you are liquid fire; connect my spirit and heart with my body and essence and my Body Realm and the physical realm and transfer it. Heat up yourself and what you carry and change it to liquid fire and frequency; put your anointing into it, which has Jesus inside of it. It is full of renewal and restoration. Flow like hot liquid, quickly and easily carrying the things from Heaven to my spirit and my heart into abundance, into my body, into my essence, into creation, into others, into the elements, into the mountains, into the seas, into the Earth, and into the Heavens. Radiate and purify the things you transfer, carry, conduct, and connect to. Everything you touch turns pure. Everything you touch is restored. Everything you touch turns to gold. Release His light, His sound, His Glory, His fire, His blood, and His living water.

We thank you that the fire of the Ancient of Days burned up any membranes or restrainers holding our beings out of place and out of order. We want these things in the measured flow of Heaven to our realms.

Blessing My Personal Realms

Acknowledge each part of your being for their respective roles in making up your whole person:

- **Spirit**, *I acknowledge you and thank you for your role in my being.*
- **Soul**, *I acknowledge you and thank you for your role in my being.*
- **Body**, *I acknowledge you and thank you for your role in my being.*

- ***Spirit***, *I charge you to fulfill your role in unity and harmony with my soul and body.*
- ***Soul***, *I charge you to fulfill your role in unity and harmony with my spirit and body.*
- ***Body***, *I charge you to fulfill your role in unity and harmony with my spirit and soul.*

- ***Father***, *I invite you to have dominion over my spirit and I yield dominion to you this day.*
- ***Jesus***, *I invite you to have dominion over my soul and I yield dominion to you this day.*
- ***Holy Spirit***, *I invite you to have dominion over my body and I yield dominion to you this day.*

Charge to the Angels

I charge the angels over my realms to work with all the angels assigned to me today and the Bond Registry Angels.

I charge the angels assigned to me to work with the Bond Registry Angels and the angels over my realms.

I charge all the angels of my realms and my personal angels to diligently labor for the fulfillment of my scrolls and blueprints.

I bless these angels in their work with Angel Elixir, Angel Food, Angel Bread, capture bags, weapons of warfare, and other items they need to fulfill their assignments.

I bless my spirit, soul, body, and Quantum Realms and instruct my spirit, soul, and body to yield to my Quantum Realms today.

Speaking to my Quantum Realms

I call my quantum emotions, (that have been restored and are the emotions of the Ancient of days) to unify with the Ancient of days.

I speak to my mind and instruct you to stand down and allow my Quantum Heart Realm to dominate.

- **Quantum Heart Realm**, *I acknowledge you and thank you for your role in my being.*
- **Quantum Emotional Realm**, *I acknowledge you and thank you for your role in my being.*
- **Quantum Essence Realm**, *I acknowledge you and thank you for your role in my being.*

- **Quantum Heart Realm**, *I charge you to fulfill your role in unity and harmony with my spirit, soul, body, Quantum Emotional Realm, and Quantum Essence Realm.*
- **Quantum Emotional Realm**, *I charge you to fulfill your role in unity and harmony with my spirit, soul, body, Quantum Heart Realm, and Quantum Essence Realm.*
- **Quantum Essence Realm**, *I charge you to fulfill your role in unity and harmony with my spirit,*

soul, body, Quantum Emotional Realm, and Quantum Heart Realm.

- **Great I AM;** *I invite you to have dominion over my Quantum Heart Realm and yield dominion to you this day.*
- **Ancient of Days:** *I invite you to have dominion over my Quantum Emotional Realm and yield dominion to you this day.*
- **El Elyon:** *I invite you to have dominion over my Quantum Essence Realm and yield dominion to you this day.*

I thank you all for the good job that you do.

Now, I call the design of Heaven to be dominant in my life.

I speak to the Glory within me to stand up, and I stand in my position as a son of the Most High God.

I also step into the Spirit of Excellence this day, and I invite the Spirit of the Lord, Wisdom, Understanding, Counsel, Might, Knowledge, and the Fear of the Lord to walk alongside me today.

I call Deep, Revelation, and Unity to walk alongside me as well.

I have put on the Righteousness of the Father and walk in Righteousness this day.

I also walk in Strength this day.

I choose also to walk with the entity Honor.

I ask the Angels of the Tuning Forks to align the frequencies of my realms.

Note

This script may be updated periodically and will appear in the corresponding blog on our website:

www.ronhorner.com

———— ∞ ————

Appendix

Silver & Gold Capture Bags

Approximately three years prior, Heaven unveiled revelations concerning capture bags for angels. This is discussed in *Dealing with Trusts & Consequential Liens*.[41] Although the capture bags are typically for containing something, in the case of the Gold and Silver Capture Bags, the Silver Capture Bags release the essence of the Father into our lives, while the Gold Capture Bags release the Glory of God. Jeremy Friedman made the correlation between the capture bags and the Quantum Essence Realm.

Here is our encounter:

A few days after seeing our first capture bag, Stephanie and I stepped into Heaven to learn more about them. We were taken to an office, and the first thing Stephanie noticed was the golden-yellow walls.

---

[41] *Dealing with Trusts & Consequential Liens* by Dr. Ron M. Horner. (LifeSpring Publishing, 2022)

Golden Glory Bags

Stephanie asked, "Lydia, will you teach us about the significance of these colors? What is the significance of this golden yellow?"

Lydia answered, "This is how glory presents itself to the human eye.

"Did you know there are Glory bags too?" she asked us.

We did not know that. "No," we answered.

Lydia continued, "There are capturing bags and bags of Glory. The angels can administer these into people's realms."

She added, "Dr. Ron, you know about the Glory and how it is administered."

Stephanie commented, "I see us taking these bags, stepping into them, and pulling them up around us. It's all-encompassing. It surrounds us.

"We can release Glory like we would release Godly bonds to people. It's something that we can release on behalf of people. You will commission their angels to bring it to them. It is a part of awakening their angels, stirring them up, and working on behalf of those who come for prayer and for ministry."

Silver Capture Bags

We had been in a ballroom in one engagement with Heaven a few days prior, and we returned there in another engagement on a different day. This time, however, only a few balls were bouncing around in the room. Stephanie saw a few balls of assorted colors lying on the floor (the same colors as some of the capture bags we had learned about previously). A silvery-looking ball captured her attention, and she knew that the silvery ball would be the topic of discussion.

Malcolm, who was with us in the ballroom, went over to the whiteboard. As we had been learning about different colors of capture bags and their uses, he correlated the color of the silver ball to silver capturing bags. He began, "This bag, too, is aerodynamic. **It swiftly contains. It does not primarily capture like the other bags you have learned about. Instead, this one, like the Glory bag, contains something to be released to others.**

This silver bag contains the essence of the Father and will bring the evidence of that in people's lives—the essence, strength, goodness, plans, needs, friendship, and value of worship of the Father.

"These are necessary things that people have been missing in their lives. The use of these bags is also for the generations. It is used in generational work."

Stephanie asked, "Can you show me more? Can you make this clearer—how is this essence of the Father and Holy Spirit used for the Body of Christ in the use of the silver capture bags? Tell me about the essence of the Father?"

Malcolm replied, "Many like the simplicities and the simplistic ways that they can utilize tools of the Kingdom. That is what these are. That is what these bags are. People can mentally and visually speak and see these things as a helpful tool on their behalf, and the simplicity of this is very helpful to them. When people pray, it is a boldness, a feeling of accomplishment, a sense of co-laboring, and a feeling that they are useful in co-laboring with angels. They are gaining strength from it, and they are seeing results."

Malcolm began showing Stephanie a picture of a person in prayer, asking the Father on behalf of the angels for the silver bags. "These are not capturing bags in the sense most of the other bags are; they are bags that contain the essence of the Father—all those things mentioned above—to be given to that person. It acts like a bonding agent, like a bond. A play on words, right?" Malcolm suggested.

Stephanie asked, "Can this be a bond that is released?"

Malcolm replied, "It is. It can be. When it is appropriate, meaning when it is relevant and opportune or an opportune time to do so. It is the right thing for the right time.

"As a simple instruction, when they are praying on behalf of someone, have them say, 'As an act of faith, take that silver bag to yourself.' Many have missed the relational side of prayer. Many can visually experience the relationship.

They can physically experience the relationship of the Father as the body uses this tool.

"This unsophisticated action shows the simplicity of Heaven, yet it is profound love and favor for the body and the people. Think of it as an act of love, and, in turn, your release of that on behalf of someone else is also an act of love—love for your neighbor, love for your friend, love for family, love for the Body of Christ.

"Use this diligently. Use it often. The essence of the Father and His love will settle upon the people. There will be a fragrance about it—an enhancement because of it, a beauty around it, and a just cause will bear witness from it. Use this in your courtroom work. It is tangible. Its immediate effects will be known because a righteous man's effective, fervent prayers will avail much.[42]

I said, "Well, let us receive the silver bag."

Stephanie began, "The silver bags, I receive it into my realms. It is tangible."

She asked Malcolm, "Is this something we can release to a struggling believer?"

"Yes," he replied. "It is very much like how a bond works. This can be released for those who do not understand this prayer paradigm, who need the essence of the Father, His love, His friendship, and it will be astounding to them."[43]

Stephanie inquired, "Malcolm if I am praying on behalf of someone and they do not know that I am praying for them, is this released?"

He responded, "Think of it as a drawing near they will experience."

She remarked, "That is good, Malcolm. It is a beautiful picture. This is like the Glory bag. I just saw myself receiving the contents of the silver bag and holding the Glory bag that I wanted to step into.

"Are they containers to be released?" she asked.

---

[42] James 5:16

[43] We can also request any of the bags for ourselves.

"Yes; these two bags are containers of the Glory of the Father and the essence and love of the Father that need to be released to people," he replied.

She inquired, "Are they also containers to gather?"

He answered, "That is right. You will utilize them to gather people into the Glory and the essence and love of the Father."

More on the Glory Bags

Stephanie said, "He is showing me that sometimes people get caught up in words when they hear people talk about the Glory. They have not ascertained how to utilize it for themselves. This is a simplistic, loving way that people can use their imaginations to utilize it for themselves and as they pray for others. Thank you for that, Malcolm."

At that moment, we briefly interrupted a situation with a client. We asked that she receive this silver bag to show her the essence of who the Father is.

As soon as Stephanie made the request, she saw her LHS (Lingering Human Spirit) Hotel[44] full of occupants, and they were requesting on behalf of themselves that the angels would bring them the silver bags while they

---

[44] Stephanie has created in her realm a gathering place for LHS's that are wanting to transition to Heaven. She refers to it as her hotel.

were at the hotel, reading their *Destiny in Heaven* book and listening to Adina's music.[45]

Malcolm handed Stephanie several silver bags and said, "You can absolutely take them to the hotel."

Stephanie asked Malcolm, "Does the gold Glory bag simply contain the Glory of God to be released to people?"

He said, "Yes. Would you like one?"

"Oh yes," I replied.

Changing subjects slightly, Stephanie asked, "Do you have more to tell us about the silver bags, Malcolm,"

Malcolm replied, "When those who struggle when they hear these messages, those who struggle with believing, falsely, that they themselves cannot ascertain the Glory or ascertain the love and the essence of the Father, these are great tools for them, for their behalf, and on their behalf. They *can* imagine. They *can see* whether they are a seer, understand what a bag looks and feels like, and imagine themselves stepping into the Glory with the tool that is the Glory bag. They *can* ascertain its essence and experience with the tool, which is the silver bag.

---

[45] This is explained in *Lingering Human Spirits – Volume 2*. (LifeSpring Publishing, 2022)

"Simplicity is needed at times, and at times, these tools are needed. Make skillful use of them, for they are for your benefit because of the Father's love. Because you have said yes to co-laboring with angels, this is a direct result and a benefit of that. It is a reminder that angels are not just useful in battle but in the presentation of the Father's love, His glory, and His Kingdom."

Stephanie observed, "Now I am in the Court of Angels, and I see all these angels with both gold and silver bags in hand.

"Can we commission you to take these silver bags to those who have drawn near the ministry?" she inquired.

The immediate answer was, "Yes!" and instantly, the angels took flight.

Ezekiel then appeared and was covered in gold dust. We asked what he had been doing and were told he had been delivering Glory bags to people on behalf of the ministry.

He began by saying, "It has been a great honor to deliver these bags and all their benefits to those that have drawn close to the ministry, especially on behalf of those who work there. It is the Father's love. The great benefit comes from loving the Father and choosing His Kingdom. These are Kingdom benefits; look at them like that. Teach the people Kingdom benefits. Align yourself with the Kingdom of Heaven. As simple as this may seem, it will work profoundly in your lives. The Father smiles down upon this ministry."

The Essence and the Glory

During another time when we engaged Heaven, we were taken upstairs to a different room, one wall of which had a view of outer space. We were seated at a table with a white flame hovering above it. Joseph, a man in white linen, said, "This is a picture of what the Essence and the Glory look like together—a pure white light."

The light then leaped off the table and into outer space.

Joseph continued, "His Glory and His essence upon the Earth, upon men's hearts, upon their realms, shall be evident just as you see the flame, just as in the day when Holy Spirit came, and flames were seen above the people.[46] The essence will rest upon the people."

Then he said, "Walk with me. As you see the rushing of the waters, you will see the Essence of the Glory light upon people."

He stopped at a brook and, referring to an engagement David, Stephanie, and I had the prior day, he said, "The baptismal pool you saw yesterday is an

---

[46] Acts 2:3

invitation, not just to Sandhills Ecclesia, but to all who draw close to the ministry, to step into the water, which contains the Essence of His Glory—there will be evidence upon their lives. You will *see* the evidence. This is the goodness of Heaven. The early believers experienced the evidence of speaking a language heretofore unknown to them. Heaven is going to do this marvelous thing."

We were then transported back to a different room. Jason, a man in white linen, was present to assist us. He brought an ancient book. On the cover was a large medallion, and Jason took a sword, inserted it into the keyhole in the medallion, and turned the sword like a key. As he did, Stephanie could hear unlocking the lock mechanism. The book was entitled *The Book of Numbers*. Stephanie asked if this was "a" book of numbers or "the" Book of Numbers. Heaven assured us it was the latter and suggested we turn to Numbers 4. Jason began helping unpack information in that passage and later in chapter 27, which spoke of inheritance. A principle of inheritance was unveiled that is simple:

---

*An inheritance may be **distributed**,*
*but **to have benefit**,*
*it must be **possessed**.*

The passage in Numbers 27 spoke of those who were to carry the presence.

Jason said, "Each of you, each of your realms, carries the tabernacle within you. You are a type and shadow of the tabernacle, the holy that lives within you—the essence—the Glory you carry within you. There are those who need this Essence and this Glory. It will shine and be evident upon each of you. They will see it. They will know it. They will want it and desire it."

Stephanie spoke up, "I have a question, Jason. Those of us who are spirit-filled and have been spirit-filled—have been carrying around the Glory and this Essence. Are you saying that what we are walking into now, this new revelation and impartation, contains new evidence of what is coming? Or what people will see?"

He replied, "The flame that they see upon you will be so evident that many will be drawn to it, and it will alight upon others."

Stephanie explained, "He just showed me a picture of how—when there is a fire, embers come off of it and go to something nearby, lighting something on fire. This is the kind of evidence we will see. Now I'm seeing an entire forest fire, but in a good way.

"Jason, this teaching, this revelation—is this about those that are or will be filled with the Holy Spirit?"

I interjected, "Since Jason is referring to the fire so much, are we referring to the baptism of the Holy Spirit *and* fire? Is that what you're alluding to?"

He confirmed, "Great question, Ron. That's exactly what this is because the Essence and the Glory create the fire. The fire is the Essence *and* the Glory combined."

Stephanie reported, "He's showing that we have learned about the Glory, and we learned yesterday about the Essence, along with the silver bags that contain the Essence. We have also been given the gold bags that contain the Glory, and he's saying, 'Imagine the two of them together,' so when we release these for people and on behalf of people, contained within them and combined together is the fire."

> *Moses brought their case before the Lord. [6] And the Lord spoke to Moses saying [7] the daughters of Zelophedad speak what is right; you shall surely give them a possession of inheritance among their father's brothers, and cause the inheritance of their father to pass to them. (Numbers 27:5-7)*

Jason said, "Just like in Numbers 27, where the Lord laid out what inheritances were for the people on our Earth, this is an inheritance. This is the truest form of inheritance from the Father—His Glory and His Essence combined, bringing the fire upon the people, lighting the fire within them, dwelling upon them, and being so evident that people are drawn to the light—to the flame."

Just then, Heaven showed us a parallel of how, in the beginning, when the Lord set up the inheritance in the natural using the Courts of Heaven, there's an inheritance for us in the spiritual.

Remember, this inheritance must not only be distributed, but it also must be possessed.

The sword of the Lord is your strength, and Wisdom is at your right hand. The Glory and the Essence that will be upon you bring the fire of the Lord.

Ezekiel then appeared with two bags over his shoulders: a gold bag on one shoulder, a silver bag on the other, and a small flame in his hand.

Stephanie asked, "Ezekiel, are you saying this is the new walk, the new beginning on behalf of this ministry for the peoples and for the Kingdom, with new insight and new understanding all gained from the seat of rest? All because He loves us?"

He replied, "This flame will be evident upon you just as it is evident in my hand. As the Father releases His glory and His essence upon the people, and as He also releases what you described as an ember, it will be a movement."

Stephanie remarked, "When he said the word 'movement,' I saw the movement of rushing water, and then I saw the movement as a frequency."

He continued, "This is what the Earth groans for. An innumerable number of angels carry this. They carry this torch. They carry this flame which is being released for such a time as this. It will grow just as a natural fire grows and spreads. This will spread. This will bring people from the North, South, East, and West."

She explained, "I just saw a picture of the whole earth and people coming from every continent and place. Do we need to commission you to do this work on behalf of the people of LifeSpring?"

"Yes," he declared.

Stephanie began:

I commission you in the name of Jesus, Ezekiel, with your commanders and ranks, on behalf of the people, those who have drawn near to the ministry, those who work for the ministry, and their families, to bring the flame that is the Essence and the Glory of the Father upon the people, that it may spread like embers and light upon the people so that all may see that it as evidence, as the Father has said that it would be in evidence.

We commission you to fully use the silver and gold bags that carry the Essence and Glory and to bring them to everyone's realms.

Father, I would like Understanding to go with this commissioning that is being released—this fire.

"Understanding plays a big part in this," she remarked. "It's the first time I've seen him as an entity that leaves and goes like that."

Continuing the commissioning, she spoke,

Father, we request that Understanding be released for all who hear, draw near, and seek the Kingdom of God. We release you, Ezekiel, your commanders, and your ranks to do this good work on behalf of the Father.

With that, Ezekiel turned and left.

Welcoming Understanding

Lydia, who had been quietly standing to the side, stepped up and said, "Speaking of Understanding,[47] much understanding will come from this. Be patient—just be patient. This is a new level, a new place. Understanding will come. Understanding is going to play a very large role at this level."

Stephanie said, "Understanding, I welcome you in everything, and just like I hold Wisdom's hand, I want to hold your hand."

Lydia continued, "There are new frequencies being released upon the Earth through these messages; frequencies that are so supernatural that Understanding being released upon them is what will bring this understanding of this frequency to their ears. Like the flame and the embers, you will see it grow among the people quickly."

---

[47] Understanding is an entity as well as a capability.

Stephanie responded, "We welcome all of this. Lydia, we welcome what Heaven has to bring through this ministry on behalf of the Kingdom of Heaven. I ask for clarity for me and for Ron, for all of this understanding as we piece this puzzle together."

Malcolm (who had been silently watching) came close. I had asked earlier if we would understand more of the capture bags we had yet to be introduced to and he had no reply. I asked him, "Is there anything else we need for the book?"

He replied, "Essence? It's an entire world." With that, he left the room.

I took a moment to look at the definition of "essence."[48] It is quite interesting:

The intrinsic nature or indispensable quality of something that determines its character, especially something abstract.

The philosophy definition was:

The inherent unchanging nature of a thing or class of things, especially as contrasted with its existence.

And also,

A property or group of properties of something without which it would not exist or be what it is.

---

[48] Google's English Dictionary definition of essence.

Another definition says,

An extract or concentrate obtained from a particular plant or other matter and used for flavoring or scent. It creates a frequency.

Yet another definition read,

The most significant element, quality, or aspect of a thing or person in concentrated form or substance as a perfume,

Also,

Something that exists, an entity.

Wikipedia[49] had an interesting definition:

Essence. It's a polysomic term using philosophy and theology as a designation for the property or set of properties that make an entity or substance what it fundamentally is and which it has by necessity and without which it loses its identity.

---

[49] Wikipedia definition of essence.

Works Cited

American Heritage Dictionary of the English Language, Fifth Edition. (2016). Houghton Mifflin Harcourt Publishing Company.

Biophoton. (2024, April 30). Retrieved from Wikipedia: https://en.wikipedia.org/wiki/Biophoton

Description

Do you want to end the conflict between your body and soul or your soul and spirit? This book will show you how. When your realms—spirit, soul, and body—understand their role in your life and are permitted to fulfill that role, life will greatly improve for you. Heaven did not stop with those three realms. We also have Quantum Realms that we need to align with to fulfill the plans the Father has for each of us.

Heaven has also provided Realm Angels to assist your realms in fulfilling their role. These understandings will take you to an entirely new place in your life. Begin today!

———— ∞ ————

About the Authors

Dr. Ron M. Horner

Dr. Ron M. Horner is an apostolic teacher specializing in the Courts of Heaven. He has written over thirty books on the Courts of Heaven, engaging Heaven, working with angels, or living from revelation.

He currently trains people in engaging the Courts of Heaven in a weekly online teaching session. You can register to participate and discover more about the Courts of Heaven prayer paradigm on his various websites, classes, products, and services found here:

www.ronhorner.com

∞

Dr. Robert Rodich, D.D., Ph.D.

Dr. Robert Rodich, D.D., Ph.D., was saved at the tail end of the Jesus movement in the early 1970s. He has been both a pastor and a Doctor of Nutrition (Alternative Medicine).

He has long been fascinated with the Quantum Realm from a biblical viewpoint. He has learned to use his expertise in that area to assist people in finding a nutritional program best suited to their specific needs. His unique method of testing energy has also opened a door to understanding the biblical supernatural realm. His focus is on biblical integrity and accuracy and the person of His Savior Jesus Christ. His life-long motto is that *it is always about Jesus*.

∞

Jeremy Friedman

Jeremy Friedman is a prophetic teacher, evangelist, intercessor, and entrepreneur with an apostolic grace. He has an amazing testimony of how God saved his life, and through his journey in finding the Lord, he has helped many others learn the heart of the Father. His prophetic gifting allows him to see the world in a unique way that often can be missed by the naked eye. Jeremy seeks the Lord daily with his whole heart to learn and receive revelation from Heaven to help build God's Kingdom here on Earth.

———— ∞ ————

About the Contributors

Rachael Testa

Rachael Testa is a wife, mother, and graduate of our CourtsNet Facilitator Training Program. She is the author of *Engaging Your Imagination for Raising Godly Children* (Scroll Publishers) and is currently working on her second book. She is pressing into Heaven to learn more about a life of sonship.

∞

Flavia Diaz

As a New Yorker, Flavia (also a graduate of our CourtsNet Facilitator Training Program) sees New York City as her domain to release the Kingdom into. We are looking forward to more insights from Flavia in the days ahead.

———— ∞ ————

Other Books

BY DR. RON M. HORNER

Building Your Business from Heaven Down

Building Your Business from Heaven Down 2.0

Building Your Business with the Blueprint of Heaven

Commissioning Angels – Volume 1

Cooperating with The Glory

Courts of Heaven Process Charts

Dealing with Trusts & Consequential Liens from the Courts of Heaven

Engaging Angels in the Realms of Heaven

Engaging Heaven for Revelation – Volume 1

Engaging Heaven for Revelation – Volume 2

Engaging Heaven for Trade

Engaging the Courts for Ownership & Order

Engaging the Courts for Your City (*Paperback, Leader's Guide & Workbook*)

Engaging the Courts of Healing & the Healing Garden

Engaging the Courts of Heaven

Engaging the Help Desk of the Courts of Heaven

Engaging the Mercy Court of Heaven

Four Keys to Dismantling Accusations

Freedom from Mithraism

Kingdom Dynamics – Volume 1

Kingdom Dynamics – Volume 2

Let's Get it Right!

Lingering Human Spirits

Lingering Human Spirits – Volume 2

Living Spirit Forward

Next Dimension Access to the Court of Supplications

Overcoming the False Verdicts of Freemasonry

Overcoming Verdicts from the Courts of Hell

Releasing Bonds from the Courts of Heaven

Unlocking Spiritual Seeing

Working with Your Realms & Your Realm Angels

SPANISH

Cómo Anular los Falsos Veredictos de la Masonería

Cómo Proceder en la Corte Celestial de Misericordia

Cómo Proceder en las Cortes para su Ciudad

Cómo Trabajar con Angeles en los Ambitos del Cielo

Cooperando con La Gloria de Dios

Las Cuatro Llaves para Anular las Acusaciones

Liberando Bonos en las Cortes Celestiales

Liberando Su Visión Espiritual

Sea Libre del Mitraísmo

Tablas de Proceso de la Cortes del Cielo

Viviendo desde el Espíritu

∞

BY JEREMY FRIEDMAN

The Ancient Pathways of Heaven

∞

BY DR. ROBERT RODICH

Moving Toward Sonship *(with Workbook)*

∞

BY RACHAEL TESTA

Engaging Your Imagination for Raising Godly Children

──── ∞ ────

Notes

Notes

Notes

Notes

Notes

Notes

www.ingramcontent.com/pod-product-compliance
Lightning Source LLC
Chambersburg PA
CBHW022002160426
43197CB00007B/234